GET MORE OUT OF LIFE—
AND PUT LESS EFFORT INTO IT!

Discover the secret shortcuts that can net you time and money while saving your hassles and heartaches. Experts in every field from health and beauty to homemaking, travel and money management let you in on:

- the fastest way to end a marriage
- the most efficient way to memorize
- the surest way to get into medical school
- the quickest way to turn off an obscene telephone caller
- the most efficient end-of-the-year tax strategies
- the most creative way to give your home a decorator look
- the best way to get rid of stress
- the most economical way to make long-distance phone calls,
  and much, much more!

SHORTCUTS

Edited by Timothy R. Augello and Gary D. Yanker

A Superlative House Book

BANTAM BOOKS
Toronto / New York / Sydney

SHORTCUTS
A Bantam Book / October 1981

ISBN: 0-553-14507-X

Published simultaneously in the United States and Canada

Bantam Books are published by Bantam Books, Inc. Its trademark,
consisting of the words "Bantam Books" and the portrayal of a
rooster, is Registered in U.S. Patent and Trademark Office and in
other countries. Marca Registrada. Bantam Books, Inc., 666 Fifth
Avenue, New York, New York 10103.

PRINTED IN THE UNITED STATES OF AMERICA

0 9 8 7 6 5 4 3 2 1

NOTE OF CAUTION

Although most of the shortcuts in this book are straightforward and foolproof, those concerning health, law, taxes and substantial investments can be more complicated, depending on individual circumstances. Here we recommend that you check with a professional before taking any serious action. Refer to advice on pages 7, 195, and 204 on how to get your money's worth from lawyers, doctors, and accountants. Also, prices on products and certain addresses are bound to change over time.

THE AUTHORS

Editors:
Timothy R. Augello and Gary D. Yanker

Administrative Editors:
Theresa Dziorney and Anne Charles

Major Contributors:

Diana Adams
R. Mark Adams
Raina Grossman
Michael Kronenwetter
Geraldine Merken

Joanna Walsh O'Neill
Seymour Roman
Harry Roman
Harry Shreiner
Richard Trubo

Other Contributors:

Michael Antonoff
Louis Botto
Din Dayal
David Gilman
Niels Johannesen
Donald B. Lane

Harriet Lesser
Bill Linn
Robert Linn
Ann Michell
J.D. Spratt
Stephen A. Stertz

Consulting Editors:

Amy Greene
Michael Manley
Jim Powell

Nick Powell
Kathi Wakefield

(See page 268 for Authors' Biographies)

ACKNOWLEDGMENTS

The editors wish to thank the following people for their assistance in the preparation of this book: Nessa Rapoport, Dian Smith, Jane Deely, Jean Blashfield Black, Ruth Wucherer, Betty Cooney, Roy Alexander, Virginia B. Schoepfer, Bob Quarteroni, Lawrence Audette, and Eleanor Berman.

TABLE OF CONTENTS

1—Health A to Z	1
2—Beauty—Top to Toe	17
3—Food	28
4—Drink	58
5—House	65
6—Indoor Gardening	107
7—Outdoor Gardening	117
8—Education and Career	139
9—Money Matters	162
10—Law	192
11—Taxes	202
12—Travel and Tourism	223
13—Recreation	245
Index	253

SHORTCUTS

INTRODUCTION

A quicker way. A more economical way. A better way. That's what all of us are seeking in our busy, hurried lives.

No one can be expert at everything. But we've contacted leading authorities in their fields—home economists, lawyers, tax consultants, doctors, gourmet cooks, botanists, investment counselors, mechanics, world travelers, and many others—and asked them to share with us the shortcuts they use in their everyday lives.

And we've searched through hundreds of volumes and articles to glean the most useful "how to" information, then capsulized it for quick and handy reference.

So if you've ever wondered how some people aways seem to accomplish so much, to manage homes and careers efficiently and well and still have time left over to enjoy life, read this book. Put this valuable information to work for you and you'll find *your* life less harried, more orderly, and ultimately more pleasant.

Chapter 1
HEALTH A TO Z

How to Stay Healthy

The best way to avoid illness is to be emotionally
well adjusted, according to a long-term study reported by Dr. George E. Valliant, a psychiatrist, in
the *New England Journal of Medicine.* Mental health
was a greater factor in physical health than smoking, drinking, obesity, and family history!

The study began in 1942 with 188 college soph-
omores and continued through almost four decades.
Such factors as stress reactions, marital stability,
and career success contributed to the emotional
states that affected physical health.

1

Fastest Acne Care

Sunlamp treatments may be fastest—but not necessarily cheapest. Three to five minutes *only* under a sunlamp for two days may correct some mild forms of acne. (The ultraviolet rays kill bacteria.) Any sunlamp treatment should be undertaken with caution.

Cheapest (and Oldest) Acne Care

Lemon juice dabbed onto each eruption. Lemon and other citruses have an astringent, drying effect.

Best Way to Age Well

There is such a thing as "retirement shock," psychologists warn. To help avoid it they suggest you educate yourself about aging beforehand. Knowledge about metabolic rates, psychic changes, and what happens to sex after sixty should relieve your worries and help you care for yourself more easily, both physically and mentally, when retirement comes. The best medication for aging is knowledge.

Best Way Not to Age at All

The so-called youth drug, Gerovital HS, is prepared and popularized by the Aslan Clinic in Rumania and duplicated in many other nations, with the exception of the United States, where it is not allowed to be sold. Gerovital, known as the "forever young" drug, is a 2 percent procaine solution with added small amounts of benzoic acid, potassium, and disodium phosphate. As one physician said, "Most of the world believes in Gerovital and clinics are popping up all over Europe, but the United States takes a dim view of it, believing that it is a fake and will not retard the aging process or prevent disorders in [the] elderly."

Easiest Way to Cope with a Common Allergy

Nickel used in costume jewelry can cause problems for some wearers, according to the American Academy of Dermatology, which says that 14 percent of all people in the United States are allergic to the metal and another 20 to 30 percent are sensitive to it.

The jewelry to watch out for is made from tin and zinc and sealed with copper and nickel, then plated with gold or silver. When the plating wears off, nickel-sensitive people can come up with a skin condition called "nickel dermatitis"—rough, red, and irritated skin. The solution? Put away your jewelry. Or have it replated.

Most Efficient Aphrodisiac

Ginseng, taken in tea or capsule form, and *gotu kola*, a tropical plant that can also be taken as a tea or in a tablet, have long been credited with the ability to harmonize the senses and the hormones. Alcohol and marijuana, on the other hand, are mere inhibition-repressors.

Simplest Way to Avoid Blisters on a Hike

Comfortable, well-fitting shoes are mandatory to prevent blisters on a long hike. Wear two pairs of socks: one thin and worn next to the skin, the other woolen. Soaping the inside of the thin pair of socks before putting them on is a useful precaution.

Best Blister Relief

Dab on a little tincture of camphor.

Quickest Way to Save Finger Sliced in a Food Processor

According to Dr. John A. Grossman, the following steps should be taken: apply pressure to the wound with a clean cloth—not a tourniquet; place any severed piece in a plastic bag and immediately put the bag in an ice-filled container; run to the nearest hospital emergency room for help. New micro-vascular surgical techniques make reimplantation possible—if the severed part is safely kept.

News in Reducing Blood Pressure

Many doctors now believe that yoga, biofeedback techniques and meditation can be quick ways of reducing hypertension in some adults. Reports from researchers state that cadmium is also a culprit adding to pressure. Cadmium is found in cigarettes, coffee, tea, white rice, and white flour. Some believe that taking zinc will reduce cadmium. Zinc in high amounts is found in brewer's yeast and wheat bran.

Best Breathing for Health

Controlled breathing reduces your pulse rate, strengthens your heart, and increases your feeling of well-being. To begin, sit cross-legged, shoulders relaxed, and inhale slowly through your nose, starting from your abdomen. Let your chest expand, ribs rise; then exhale slowly through your mouth. Practice for a few minutes every day until proper breathing is second nature.

Easy Caffeine Check

If your physician says you should cut down on caffeine, you must first realize that caffeine is not only found in coffee but in tea, which has about half the caffeine of coffee. In a 5-ounce (150 milligrams) cup of coffee, there are 83 milligrams of caffeine. A 5-ounce cup of tea (the tea-bag type) has 42 milligrams of caffeine. A good way to avoid caffeine completely is to drink Postum, the coffee-flavored drink that tastes like the real thing but is made of grain, molasses, and other caffeine-free products.

Most Efficient Balm for Chapped Lips

Beeswax, available at your drugstore, is a major ingredient in most commercial balms. Rub a small amount of the soft, gummy substance onto your lips as needed.

Easy Cholesterol Cutting

Any doctor will tell you that if your pet passion is ice cream, you are consuming a high-cholesterol food. The way to cut down is to eat the less expensive brands, which contain less butterfat. Or eat ice milk.

Cure for Sore Throat

Make your own syrup. It will be just as effective as most and cheaper than over-the-counter preparations. Mix 1 part syrup cerasi (cherry syrup), 2 parts glycerine (both of these can be obtained at your pharmacy), and 1 part concentrated lemon juice. Add a glob of honey and shake well. A great remedy for the "raspies."

Most Efficient Way to Prevent Dandruff

A small amount of zinc, used to treat many skin diseases (of which dandruff is one), can be added to a mild shampoo when necessary. You can also try dandruff shampoos, but switch brands frequently— the body quickly gets used to medications.

Most Radical Way to Cure Depression

The quickest way to get into fits of depression for some people is to live in a place that has hot spells, say researchers at Johns Hopkins University, who interviewed 900 people living in all sorts of weather. Extreme depression and heat are partners, and when you are subject to them you also are more likely to have accidents or become ill. Remedy? Move!

Cheapest Dental Care

Most large teaching hospitals with a dental school also have a dental clinic where their students work (under expert supervision) at rates generally lower than those of dentists in private practice. An additional advantage: students have access to the most up-to-date equipment and expertise. Drawbacks: you may not see the same dentist each time; supervision of all work by faculty members can be time-consuming.

Most Efficient All-Around Dental Care

Preventive dentistry. More and more dentists and dental hygienists are taking time to explain the principles of brushing, flossing, and their role in "dental awareness." It's all designed to stop problems *before* they start.

Fastest Teeth-Cleaning Device Used by Dentists

"Cavitron," which operates on ultra-high frequency sound waves, vibrates plaque and calculus off your teeth. It's particularly good for built-up layers of the residue.

Best Tooth Replacement

If you loose a tooth through injury, there's a chance it could be surgically replanted if you are careful to follow the accepted medical procedure: clean the tooth and immediately place it back into its socket. Hold it in with a wire, chewing gum, or wax—or if this isn't possible, put it in ice water with a pinch of salt until you can rush it to an implant surgeon's office or to a hospital.

Most Efficient Deodorant

Chlorophyll, taken in tablet form as directed on the bottle, purifies the system and reduces odors almost before they start. A daily serving of parsley, high in cholorophyll, is also helpful.

Most Efficient Way to Find a Doctor

Almost every county in the nation has its own medical society. (Live in a county too small to maintain one? Try the next largest county.) Anyone who calls the county medical society for information is told the name, hospital affiliation (if any), type of certification, and gender of the nearest medical doctors. It's then up to you to contact the doctors and ask *questions* about anything you think would affect your medical care. For example, does the doctor make house calls? Does he or she have office hours that fit your schedule? What types of medical coverage are involved? Any doctor will be willing to answer your questions in advance.

Best Time to Enter a Hospital

Short of an emergency, the best time to enter a hospital is probably midweek or after a holiday. On Fridays things slow down for the weekend and routine tests and other procedures may be put off until Monday. If you enter on Monday, you'll be last on the list until the staff catches up on priorities.

Any time, be sure your own peculiarities and problems are made known to everyone around, even at the risk of antagonizing people. If you're allergic to milk products, for example, then the meals you get served should reflect the fact. Don't be afraid to speak up.

Quick Medicaid Information

If you are a senior citizen, you should be up on what's happening in Medicaid laws that affect you. For information write: Health Care Financing, HEW, 330 C Street SW, Washington, D.C. 20201. The booklet will be sent to you free.

Fastest Way to Distinguish Between Psychiatrists and Psychologists

Psychiatry is a medical specialization; its practitioners have an M.D. degree and can prescribe medication. A psychologist (usually) has a Ph.D. or an Ed.D. degree and may be trained in a variety of techniques and procedures. Ask any doctor about his or her methods *before* beginning treatment.

Cheapest Psychiatric Care

Contact your local community health center. Most centers will be able to direct you to a clinic where payment is scaled according to what you earn. (Remember: reduced rate doesn't mean reduced services.)

Cheapest Drugs

Generic ones—that is, the compound itself without a company "brand name" or packaging. Most doctors don't prescribe generic drugs unless asked to by the patient, so it pays to ask. Also, how you comparison shop is as important as where you do it. In a study of pharmacy pricing practices, the Washington, D.C., Public Interest Research Group found that fourteen out of the eighteen pharmacies they contacted quoted different—usually lower—prices over the phone from those they gave in person.

Cheapest Drugs For Those Over 55

The American Association of Retired Persons—open to anyone over 55—offers members a discount on drugs. For further information write: 555 Madison Avenue, New York, New York 10022.

Cheapest Medical Resource

Water. Drink it cold to help cleanse the internal system and prevent constipation. Drink it hot to stimulate the gastric juices and also provide some relief from nausea, vomiting, and even indigestion.

Most Efficient Way to Prevent Ear Infection While Swimming

Coat small wads of cotton with petroleum jelly. Place in each ear before swimming. The jelly is a more effective moisture barrier than ear plugs. (And if you're worried about ear infection, remember that fresh or salt water swimming is preferable to pools, where chlorine can irritate ears and eyes.)

Fastest Way to Decide Between Hard and Soft Contact Lenses

Do you plan to wear your lenses for long stretches at a time? If so, get hard lenses. They're small and must be fitted exactly to your eye, but they're better for long periods of wear—and cost less. (Approximately $175 compared to $225 for soft lenses.)

Sunglass Test

To buy stylish sunglasses and be sure they won't harm your eyes, turn the glasses over in the store so that the fluorescent overhead lighting reflects on the inside of the glass lens. If after you move the glasses slightly (so that the reflection travels across the lens) the image is not wavery or distorted, you have a good lens!

Most Efficient Glasses Cleaner

A little piece of damp newspaper works as well or better than cloths or tissues, which can scratch lenses.

Fastest Vision Aid for Those Over 60

Turn on more light! The average 60-year-old needs seven times as much light as the average 20-year-old to perform the same tasks, says the American Optometric Association, which also advises incandescent (yellow) rather than fluorescent (blue) light for older eyes.

Fastest Way to Distinguish Between Opthamologists, Optometrists, and Opticians

Opthamology is a medical specialty concerned with the structure and function of the eye; its practitioners have an M.D. degree and can prescribe medication and perform surgery. An optometrist is primarily concerned with vision rather than the eye itself. An optician makes corrective lenses.

Most Efficient Way to Prevent Foot Problems

Never wear the same shoes or socks two days in a row.

Summer Foot Comfort

All-cotton socks. They let your feet breathe in hot weather and reduce foot perspiration.

Best Shoes for Everyday

- Make sure that the sole of the shoe is wide enough for the sole of your foot.
- Make sure the arch fits your foot properly. Obviously, if you have a high arch, the arch of the shoe must be high to give you support. A foot with a low arch needs a lower-arched shoe.
- The shoe should have a toe box big enough to permit you to wiggle your toes.
- Make certain that the shoe has a straight inside last, so that your inside heel and big toe are in a straight line.

Best Shoes for Women

Shoes with low heels. The medical profession universally recommends avoiding high heels, saying they throw your entire body off balance. To walk in high heels, you have to bend your knees, your lumbar region has to make an arch, and your neck cranes forward.

High heels also prevent your feet from performing their shock-absorbing function, which affects the joints from your legs and back up to your neck.

Most Efficient Way to Dress for Freezing Weather

Wear several loose layers of clothing. But avoid adding that extra shirt or sweater, it could cut off the circulation air needed to retain body warmth. And remember this: if you dress *too* warmly for the cold you'll become overheated. The resulting perspiration can dampen your clothing and as it evaporates, cool down your body.

Best Way to Raise Body Heat in Winter

Outside of exercise, nothing helps raise your body temperature better than an increase in the amount of calories, especially protein and fat, in your diet.

Cheapest Way to Prevent Frostbite

Warm coldest parts against your own—or another—body. For example, place cold hands under your arms or cover your nose with the inside of the elbow.

Fastest Cure for a Hangover

Pure oxygen. A few blasts and the hangover is blown away. Not very practical for most people, however, so . . .

Cheapest Cure for a Hangover

Sleep. Stay in bed and sleep it off. But this is often impossible, given the demands of life, so . . .

Most All-Around Practical Cure for a Hangover

Take two aspirin and a lot of water before going to bed. In the morning, take two Alka Seltzer in a tall glass on ice; clears the head, settles the stomach, gets you going.

Cheapest Cure for Hiccups

Breathe into a paper bag as many times as you can. The action helps to balance the oxygen/carbon dioxide levels in your system. It was an imbalance that started your diaphragm contracting in the first place, producing hiccups.

Fastest and Cheapest Hive Remedy

An ice cube, applied on the first sign of a hive. The cold reduces swelling—and itching.

Cheapest Indigestion Relief

For occasional upsets, sprinkle a little table salt in a glass of seltzer water. The "salt-seltzer" that results is similar to the commercial brands—only cheaper—and without added ingredients like aspirin that can upset your stomach.

Cheapest Appetizer and Digestive Aid

Fresh ginger tea.

Most Efficient Way to Reduce Flatulence

Before eating that next big bowl of beans, add a few slices of ginger and/or a teaspoon of savory.

Best Way to Cure Insomnia

If you can't sleep, try eating! L-Tryptophane is an amino acid found in milk and cheese, which are two terrific sleep inducers simply because of the secret ingredient. Having a cheese sandwich and a glass of milk is much safer and often more effective than taking some of those over-the-counter pills which are supposed to help you see the Sandman.

Cheapest Relief of Menstrual Cramps

A cup of raspberry leaf tea, made with only a tablespoon of the herb (approximate cost: 15¢ a cup).

Most Natural Mouthwash

Fennel, sprinkled in warm water as a mouthwash or mixed with baking soda as a toothpaste. (Fennel is also used to flavor Italian sausage, but don't worry—it has a less pungent effect when applied directly to your mouth.)

Cheapest Relief of Nausea

Cola syrup has been prescribed for the relief of nausea and vomiting for a good number of years. Many physicians prescribe it as a first step in relieving nausea, as the syrup from the kola bean is a well known antispasmodic. Simply ask for a container (about 50¢ worth) of cola syrup and take two teaspoons every 10 minutes until the upset subsides.

Best Way to Stop Nosebleeds

Sit and do nothing, with your head bent slightly forward. If possible, gently press cotton against your nostrils. Most nosebleeds stop quickly by themselves, and rubbing or otherwise touching the sensitive nose only makes things worse. If nosebleeds occur more than once in a short period of time, call your doctor.

Poison Ivy Emergency Treatment

Wash with yellow soap and water, then alcohol. Cover with paste of laundry soap and water, or with Calamine lotion. Allow to crust and dry on skin. Do not scratch—this will spread the poison!

Fastest Way to Clear Sinuses

Gently sniff a mild solution of salt water from your cupped hand. Close off the right nostril and sniff up the left, then reverse. ("Gently" is the key word here—the membranes of the nose are sensitive.)

Quick Sneeze Prevention

If you *must* stop a sneeze, gently rub that little fold between your nose and upper lip. It's what's known as a shiatsu point in acupressure, the Japanese form a massage. Rubbing this point acts on the nervous system to deactivate sneeze impulse.

Most Efficient Splinter Remover

Fill a wide-mouthed bottle to the top with boiling water. Place the splintered spot over the mouth of the bottle and press down—*hard*. The pushing will draw the skin away from the splinter and the heat of the water will pull it out. *Without* a needle.

How to Handle a Bee Sting

If you're stung by a bee or a yellowjacket, don't pull the stinger out, because that could result in more venom being squeezed into the flesh. Health departments suggest scraping away the poison sac with your fingernail or a knife, then washing the area with soap and water and applying a cold compress. A slice of onion applied to the sting, after the bee's stinger has been carefully removed, can work wonders. So can vinegar (although this is not for bee stings) or mud packs made of earth and any available cold liquid. If you have a violent reaction to a sting, as many people do, and if you have any of the following symptoms—sneezing, diarrhea, dizziness, cramps, upset stomach, fainting, shortness of breath, or swelling of the joints, see a physician quickly!

Best Stress Reliever

Swimming. Doctors say swimming works out every muscle in your body, stimulates the cardiovascular system, and is psychologically very relaxing. Try to increase the distance you swim each day.

Cheapest Way to Relax

It doesn't cost anything to practice meditating, which is the best way to relax and relieve tension. Set aside a time and a place free of interruption. Sit in a comfortable position. Close your eyes, relax your muscles, and breathe deeply. Repeat a word or phrase of your choice in order to break the train of distracting thoughts. It takes a few times to get used to it, but meditation has been proven medically effective, so persevere.

Best Natural Sunburn Remedy

Nature's remedy for sunburn hurt and most other burns is the aloe cactus, if you live near a desert or a store that carries it. The true aloe has succulent leaves containing a fluid that, according to doctors, is a miracle of nature.

This creamy fluid can be applied to any part of your body, even sensitive areas of your face, to relieve burns. It feels cool and draws out heat and pain. The aloe is easy to grow and can be propagated at any time of the year from suckers which grow at its root line. The plant, if you wish to grow one, is known as the *aloe vera*.

Cheapest Sunburn Lotion

The tannic acid in tea makes it an excellent soothing remedy for sunburn. For obvious reasons, iced tea is better than hot tea for this purpose.

Cheapest Toothpaste

You can make a cheaper and better toothpaste with 1 part glycerine and 2 parts powdered pumice mixed well with oil of peppermint or even Scope mouthwash or some other brand. All ingredients may be purchased at your drugstore.

Cheapest Tooth Powder

The cheapest tooth powder on the market—and every bit as effective as the most expensive—is ordinary baking soda!

Chapter 2
BEAUTY—TOP TO TOE

Most Efficient Hair Care Schedule

Shampooing depends on hair texture, say experts, who suggest every day for extremely oily hair, every second day for oily hair, every four or five days for normal hair, and once a week for dry hair. Likewise, if you "steam" your face—every two weeks is plenty.

Tips About Hair

- If you have frayed, split ends you cannot truly "recondition" them; the best thing is to cut your hair back to a healthier level.
- The only function of "conditioners" is to add sheen, antistatic action, and manageability.
- Don't worry about moderate hair loss . . . you shed about a hundred hairs a day.

17

- The best shampoos are mild, like those made for babies. It is rinsing that is most important. If it takes you five minutes to shampoo, it should take you ten minutes to rinse.
- Vigorous brushing and scalp massage only take away the outer layer of dirt and impurities hair accumulates.
- The healthiest hair is cared-for hair. Waving, bleaching, straightening, dyeing, and curling hair weakens it. So always be extra careful about what you use on your hair and how it reacts to products.

Most Efficient Way to Brush Hair

Bend over at the waist and let your head hang down. Brush your hair from the base of your neck out. This method helps stimulate and equalizes oils needed for shine and growth.

Fastest Hairdo

Any hairdo that's cut closest to the shape of your head. Let your hair tell you (and your hairdresser) which way it wants to fall, flip, or curl—then let it. The best hairdos have the same shape wet as they do dry.

Shampoo Stretcher

Buy the best shampoo and add a half-packet of plain gelatin (mixed with water according to directions). This pushes up the protein content of the shampoo, always important, and adds to the volume.

Cheapest Dry Shampoo

No need to buy those expensive dry shampoos for in-between washings. For a fast way to get rid of the greasies when shampooing is inconvenient, use ordinary talcum powder. Apply a little to your hair and brush through. Just remember, a little goes a long way.

Cheapest Hair Conditioners

Apply a beaten egg white mixed with half a mashed avocado (honest!) to your hair. Massage, then rinse with warm—not hot—water. (Hot water on an egg preparation tends to thicken it.)

Bargain Setting Lotion

Use a tiny amount of unflavored gelatin dissolved in boiling water for hair sets—it works!

Cheapest Way to Prevent Baldness

It's a matter of heredity, a well-balanced diet, all-around good health and a lot of good luck. But you can also keep more hairs on your head by remembering never to brush or comb hair while it's wet—it's much more likely to loosen and, in time, fall out.

An Exercise Facial

Throw your head back and slowly open and close your mouth. Repeat. Then clench your teeth and smile as widely as you can. Hold for several seconds. Relax and repeat. Both exercises increase flexibility and circulation.

Quick Massage

Fill a paper cup with water and place in the freezer. When it's chilled, cut about an inch from the bottom of the cup and run the protruding ice over your skin. But remember, never let the ice remain directly on your skin for more than a moment. Keep it moving in a circular or up-and-down motion, or cover it with a clean washcloth and reapply.

Cheapest Facial

Cold water, applied with 20 vigorous splashes (approximately 2 minutes), improves circulation.

For a more expensive, classier splash: chilled Perrier, Evian, or other bottled water on a cotton ball.

Kitchen Facial

Separate one egg. Avoiding the eye area, lather your face with egg white and wait for it to dry. When the mask is set, apply the yolk to soften and remove it. Then rinse with cool water. Albumen (egg white) is loaded with vitamin B, and the yolk is an excellent source of A and D, all beneficial to the skin.

For a more elaborate version: make a paste of an egg yolk, a pinch of alum, a tablespoon of fuller's earth, and a teaspoon of honey. Spread liberally on your face. Leave for 20 minutes, then rinse off with cold water.

Cheapest Freshener or Toner

For an effective and inexpensive toner, mix witch hazel and distilled water and apply to your skin. (Keep away from your eyes.) Half and half may be a good way to start out. Increase or decrease the witch hazel content depending on your skin type. Your homemade skin tightener will be even more effective if you keep it in the refrigerator. This is especially pleasant to skin in hot weather.

Cheapest (and Oldest) Freckle Remedy

Apply lemon juice mixed with a little honey onto freckles once a week after a thorough washing, and stay out of the sun.

Fastest Way to "Set" Makeup

Fill a plant sprayer with chilled tap water and spray quickly over your face.

Most Efficient Way to End Eye Puffiness

Place cold camomile tea bags on your eyes. Lie down for 20 minutes and watch your eyestrain and puffiness diminish. Or try a thick slice of raw potato on each eye. The starch helps reduce puffiness and bags.

Fastest Way to Get Rid of Bags Under Your Eyes

Smooth a little Preparation H under your eyes, avoiding the lash area, to reduce swelling quickly. It works on hemorrhoids and will also work on puffs beneath the eye. Doctors' wives have known about this trick for years.

Cheapest Way to Get Rid of Bags Under Your Eyes

Fight bags with bags—tea bags, that is. Save your used tea bags. When you need a quick answer to puffy eyes, wet the bags in lukewarm water, lie down, and apply under your eyes. You should see a difference in about 20 minutes. The scientific reasoning is that tannic acid helps reduce swelling.

Fastest Way to Give Your Face a Lift

Next time you're having your hair tinted, ask your hairdresser to apply some tint to your eyebrows too. Most faces don't need the shadows cast by dark or heavy brows. (But don't try it at home. Expert hands are needed to keep the tint out of your eyes.)

Fastest Way to Make Eyelashes Look Thicker

Apply mascara as usual. Wait for it to semi-dry and then dust your lashes lightly with loose face powder. Then apply another coat of mascara. The result? Instant thickness.

Cheapest Lash Lengthener

A smidgen of olive oil, touched lightly to your lashes every night before retiring.

Fastest Nose Job

No surgery is required to make your nose look shorter, straighter, or narrower. It's a trick done with mirrors—and makeup. To minimize a bump, draw a straight line down the center of your nose with Max Factor's white Erace, or a similar product. Use your finger to blend in the color. For a narrower look, apply darker makeup base to the sides of the nose. And for fast shortening, put a touch of blusher on the tip.

Lipstick Repair

Heat the ends just enough with a lighted match so that the broken halves can be joined and pressed together.

Best Way to Conceal a Double Chin

A tiny bit of darker foundation applied in a triangle directly beneath the jawline can make a double chin less obvious.

Soap Saver

A small piece of aluminum foil applied to the underside of your favorite soap will keep it from resting in water and make it last much longer.

Fastest Cure for Round Shoulders

Bend over at the waist until your upper body is parallel with the floor. Fling your arms up and down ten times. Repeat two or three times a day. Gradually add weights to hands, up to two or three pounds. The strengthened muscles between your shoulder blades will help your posture greatly. Also, breathe deeply, chin up, and remember to keep your shoulders back.

Most Efficient Way to Increase Bustline

The breasts themselves are mainly glands and

fatty tissues that don't respond to exercise the way muscles do. A stronger, firmer bustline, however, can result from a carefully designed weight-lifting program, which will strengthen the pectoral muscles supporting the breasts. Check with your local gym: you can't start lifting weights without guidance.

Cheapest Way to Eliminate Elbow Roughness

Rub a lemon on your elbows. It softens roughness and bleaches the skin.

Speedy End to Dishpan Hands

Apply plenty of hand cream before you put on rubber gloves to do dishes. The warmth of the water will help the cream soften your skin.

Easy Nail Care

Always file fingernails in one direction. Use an emery board, never a metal file; the metal snags your nails. For short nails, buffing is the best method. It's very healthy and helps circulation.

Office Girl's Exercise for a Flatter Derriere

Stand 12 to 18 inches from your desk and place your hands on top. Keep your upper body straight and slowly raise one leg backward and as high as possible. Return to starting position, alternate legs and repeat several times.

Cheapest Foot Moisturizer

Put a small amount of vegetable shortening on your heels or other dry skin areas—and snuggle into a pair of white socks. The shortening acts as a fast and inexpensive skin softener.

Easiest Way to Cure Itchy, Dry Skin

Bathe every other day with ½ cup boric acid in

a tub full of water. Dermatologists advise against bathing every day in winter if you have dry skin.

Cheapest Way to Prevent Skin from Wrinkling in Bathtub

Apply a little petroleum jelly to the skin *before* bathing. Enough will remain on delicate portions of the skin to prevent that "prune-y" look. Avoid taking long baths.

Cheapest Night Cream

A jar of petroleum jelly. The chief benefit of any moisturizer, however expensive, is that it seals in your body's natural moisture. Nothing does this more effectively than petroleum jelly, which can be found in any supermarket.

Cheapest Body Lotion

Baby oil. Smoothed on after a bath while your skin is still damp, it helps retain natural moisture and has a softening effect.

A tiny bit patted on the face, hands, and elbows can protect skin and add needed moisture. (Note: if you have naturally oily skin, adding baby oil may cause blemishes. In that case, just put it around your eyes and on your neck.)

Cheapest Perfume

Add a drop of musk scent to your baby oil and dab on your wrists and inner elbows. The scent will cling to the oil and last longer.

Most Efficient Way to Choose a Perfume

Spray each of three fragrances on separate cotton balls. (Use the sample sprays available in large department stores and don't try more than three—it confuses the nose.) The cotton ball will tell you the dominant fragrance in the perfume.

Interested? Find out how it will smell on you. Dab each of the three on different parts of your body. Spend an hour doing something else, then sniff again. Now you'll learn the underlying fragrance of the perfume, how long it lasts, and how well it reacts to your body heat. If you like it now, go back and buy it—but in the form of cologne. It's cheaper than perfume, in case you change your mind after you've worn it several times. Once you're sure it's you, you can invest in the perfume whose scent stays active longer.

Cheapest Exercise Mat

The one you make yourself, from a piece of 1-inch-thick polyurethane foam, 30 inches wide by 70 inches long. Cover foam with a zippered envelope you make from a sheet or length of bright cotton duck and attach long ribbons to each end. Roll it up, tie it, and take it wherever you go so that you never miss your daily workout.

Cheapest Exercise

A length of rope. Used as a jumprope, it is an tired. excellent cardiovascular aid. And with one end made stationary, it can be used for a variety of isometric strength exercises.

Most Efficient Exercise

Walking. Not only does it use practically every muscle, it also improves circulation, helps the heart, and increases stamina. Walking at 3½ miles an hour also burns off more calories (182) than skating (118) or cycling (95). If you walk 30 minutes about 180 times during the year, you should be able to take off about 20 pounds in 12 months!

Easy Water Exercise

At the beach: to strengthen thigh and leg muscles run every day in thigh-high water until you're tired. Each day you'll be able to run a little farther. The resistance of the water will give your muscles a real workout.

At the pool: grasping the handrail firmly with one hand, swing your other arm in wide circles over and through the water, ten times forward, ten times backward. Alternate and repeat five times. Good for upper arm muscles.

Gardener's Exercise

As you're kneeling and planting or weeding: with your feet touching, arms straight out, press your knees into the earth while trying to bring them together. Hold for the count of five, repeat ten times. Result: firmer upper thighs.

Fastest Way to Curb Your Appetite

Exercise just before eating. Exercise temporarily depresses the appetite. It also takes up time that might be spent eating and promotes a feeling of well-being that makes dieting easier.

Cheapest Clothes to Care For

Buy clothes made of washable, wrinkle-resistant fabrics that don't require either dry-cleaning or ironing. Not only are clothes made out of such materials often cheaper initially, they are much cheaper to care for—and over the life of a garment, the costs of care can add up to much more than the cost of the garment itself.

Cheapest Hosiery

Panty hose and knee-highs purchased in five-and-dime stores, supermarkets, and discount stores are made by the same manufacturers who turn out the expensive brands. Even the small defects in products labeled "seconds" seldom affect wear.

Economical Evening Glitter

Sew shining sequins or colorful feathers to a small wool cap in black or a bright color or outline the pattern in the ends of a silk scarf with sequins.

SPECIALLY FOR MEN

Best Shave for a Man

Triple lathering and a light shave, rather than a single lathering and an intense shave, is best according to a leading New York dermatologist. This method gives a good shave with little friction-burn irritation.

Rule of Thumb for Sleeve Length

As a general rule, jacket sleeves should end about 4½ to 5 inches from the tip of the thumb.

Best Raincoat

One with a set-in one-piece sleeve is recommended, so that the coat lies smoothly across the shoulders. Also make sure that the fabric is yarn-dyed so that it has life and vibrancy.

Chapter 3
FOOD

SHOPPING

Shopping Efficiently

Rising food costs are a bane to everyone's budget, yet most people could still pay substantially less than they do for their groceries. The following tips can help keep costs down:

Watch for sales. Supermarkets regularly offer sales coupons in newspapers, often on Wednesdays and Thursdays. These coupons can provide savings of up to 34 percent. Buying sale-price items in quantity and storing or freezing stretches the savings.

Buy generics and house brands. Generic foods, those sold without brand names, can subtract an impressive amount from your food bill. Savings can be as high as 40 percent off the cost of name brands, somewhat less off the cost of the so-called "house" brands sold under the brand name of the store rather than the manufacturer. The U.S. Office of Consumer Affairs warns, however, that although claims are sometimes made that the low prices for generic foods are made possible by their plain packaging and lack of advertising, only about 1 percent of the savings come from these factors. For the most part, the huge savings come from lower quality. This doesn't mean that the products aren't good, just that they are apt to be of a somewhat lower quality than the higher-priced name brands. Try them. You may well find that the savings are worth whatever sacrifice in quality is involved. Experiment to discover what brands you can change without any significant difference— cleaners and dishwashing soaps, for example, or canned foods you intend to cook with.

Most Economical Way to Buy Food

For those who can afford the time and have a food store in their neighborhood, the most economical way to purchase food is the opposite of what you might think: daily buying exactly what you need for each day's meals. It actually costs less than quantity buying.

Daily specials can mean important savings; and unless the household is larger than four people, buying in bulk often results in both waste and spoilage. A 5-pound roast of beef, for example, is rarely eaten without waste in the average household.

Most Efficient Food-Shopping Schedule

For greater safety and to extend the storage life of your food purchases to the maximum, try to shop in the following order: start with nonfood items such as paper towels and detergents; then pick up canned and bottled goods; follow those with fresh vegetables; then meat; and just before you go

to the checkout counter, frozen foods. Go straight
home and put your purchases away in reverse order,
starting with the frozen foods and leaving the
nonfood items until the end. This schedule will
maximize food quality and minimize any possible
spoilage.

How to Get More for Your Money

The shoppers' scales in the supermarket produce
department are there for you. Use them!

You may find, for example, that the bagged onions and potatoes are less than the weight reported
(or more!), that there are wide variations in the
weights of lettuce heads (all sold at the same price),
that prepackaged tomatoes, celery, and carrots come
in different weights. . . .

At the other side of the store, in the dairy department, eggs are sold by size—which also means
weight. If there is a difference of 9¢ or more between "medium" and "large," or "large" and "extra
large," get the smaller size. There isn't a 9¢ difference in the total weight of the eggs themselves.

Buy the Contents, Not the Packages

Keep an eye on the *weights* of the items you buy.
Boxes of approximately the same size can contain
food items in widely varying quantities for approximately the same prices.

Cheapest Way to Learn about Canned Foods

A contact with the local U.S. Department of Agriculture office or a letter to the Department of
Agriculture, Food Safety and Quality Service, Information Division, Room 1078 South Building,
Washington, D.C. 20250, will bring sample of "FSQS
Facts," a pamphlet describing what the consumer
can expect to find in canned goods. This includes
quantities, number of servings per can, and content
percentages prescribed by law. The pamphlet is free.

Bargain Buys in Canned Foods

Dented cans that are offered at reduced prices are good buys. The dents are the result of careless handling, not spoilage. The cans to avoid are those which bulge. If you ever spot a bulging can on your own shelf, discard it immediately.

How to Open a Can

If you open all cans on the bottom, you get everything that has settled, it comes out easier, and—in case you forgot to rinse the can—bottoms are almost always cleaner than tops.

Home Slicing

Doing it yourself saves money. Block or wedge cheese can be sliced at home, and it costs less than if purchased already sliced. Same with unsliced meats like salami. Your food will keep longer too.

Cheapest Way to Locate Unusual Foods

If you have reason to locate a seller of unusual foods—like goat meat or turtle eggs—you can probably find an association of the growers or distributors of the item in question in the public library. Gale's *Encyclopedia of Associations* lists all American associations for whatever purpose; and American food growers and purveyors all have associations, including the pet-food manufacturers and breeders of Highland cattle (a long-haired bovine suited to rocky and cold terrain).

COOKING BASICS

Most Efficient Cooking Information

Almost all food packages tell you how best to prepare the contents. Don't ignore these instructions just because they come with the product. Experi-

enced cooks know that even a fairly common product like noodles is best cooked exactly as the
manufacturers recommend because that is the way
the product has been tested in their own kitchens
or testing facilities.

Most Energy-Efficient Way to Check if Food is Done

Whenever possible, time your cooking with a clock
or use a timer. Frequently opening the oven door
to see how the food is doing prolongs cooking time
and wastes energy.

Most Efficient Recipe File

After going to all the trouble of copying a recipe,
don't allow wet or greasy fingers to make it un-
readable. Coating the card with transparent shellac
will make the card resist stains and be easy to
clean.

Cheapest Food Cooler

You can make your own inexpensive picnic cooler
out of two cardboard boxes and some newspaper.
Take two cardboard boxes that are approximately 3"
to 4" different in size. Put the smaller box into the
larger, lining the bottom of the larger box with a
1-inch thickness of newspaper and filling in the
spaces between the boxes' sides with newspaper
too. The newspaper will provide insulation for the
inner box. Then put ice in a plastic bag, and food or
beverages to be cooled in the inner box.

EGGS

Most Efficient Grade of Egg

This depends on how you're going to use it. For
baking or other uses in which looks and taste quality are not most important, Grade AA will do fine.

For frying or garnishing a sandwich, when t. and texture are essential, better buy Fancy.

Don't Shell Out More for Eggs . . .

In areas where brown eggs and white eggs are sold, buy the cheapest in the size you prefer. There's no difference in taste.

Low Cost Eggs

When eggs are on sale, take full advantage. Buy dozens and freeze them. Eggs may be frozen whole but they must be placed in containers that allow ½ to ¾ inch of space around each one as they expand. Use rigid containers or just a plastic freezer box and they will last up to nine months. To thaw, place them in the container in your fridge.

How to Boil an Egg Without Breaking

Prick the large end of the egg with a needle or egg pricker, thus allowing air to escape during cooking.

Quickest Way to Cook an Egg

A droplet of vinegar in the pan with cooking eggs—any style—will help the eggs firm up and make them cook faster and more evenly.

When Is an Egg a Hard-Boiled Egg?

Spin the egg on a counter top. A hard-boiled egg will whirl around as smoothly and quickly as a top. An uncooked egg will wobble.

Easiest Way to Peel a Hard-boiled Egg

When egg is hard-boiled, plunge it immediately into cold water and leave until chilled. Then crack the shell in a band around the middle, peel off bits, and pull away both ends. A teaspoon of vinegar in the boiling water also makes eggs easier to peel.

; Treat

the crusts of bread slices, butter both
ch slice and fit one per cup into big
muffin tins. Break egg on top of each slice and
cover loosely with aluminum foil. Then bake and
enjoy.

Professional Omelet

Never add milk to your omelet mixture. Famed
chefs say the pro way is to add a small amount of
water instead. Both milk and salt may make the
omelet turn out rubbery. Also, take the eggs out of
the refrigerator 45 minutes before using.

For a super fluffy omelet try this French chef
method: add a pinch of cornstarch to the egg mix.
It keeps the eggs from collapsing and makes the
omelet as fluffy as a summer cloud.

Fastest Route to an Elegant Lunch

An omelet. Nothing could be easier or faster than
a savory omelet served with a green salad and a
glass of chilled white wine. Here are some fillings
you can whip up easily:

• Frozen chopped spinach with sour cream.
• Mushrooms sautéed in butter with sherry added.
• Blend cherry tomatoes (you can use large ones,
  but press out most of the watery juice), grated
  cheddar cheese, and fresh basil.
• Diced avocado, shredded Swiss cheese, or Jack
  cheese and diced chicken or turkey.
• Zucchini, which has been sautéed in olive oil with
  a clove of garlic, and a generous sprinkling of
  Parmesan cheese.
• Whipped cottage cheese blended with sliced ripe
  olives and chopped cherry tomatoes.

How to Poach a Pretty Egg

Pierce a hole in the large end of the egg to prevent cracking and lower it gently into boiling water for 10 seconds. Then prepare as usual—egg white will coagulate slightly and hold its shape while poaching.

How to Separate an Egg

Use your own fingers. Slightly cup and spread your fingers, pour the egg onto your fingers. The white goes through; the yolk doesn't.

MILK

Secret Way to Keep Milk Longer

To keep milk longer buy it in the carton rather than in glass or plastic, says Dr. Paul Dimick, a food scientist at Penn State University. Cardboard blocks out most of the fluorescent light used in store displays, which can give milk a bad taste and destroy valuable riboflavin (vitamin B_2). In tests on milk refrigerated at 45 degrees and exposed to fluorescent light for 72 hours, milk in cardboard containers suffered no flavor alteration, and only 10 percent of the riboflavin was lost. In glass containers, the milk lost 27 percent of its riboflavin and had an off-flavor in 6 hours. Plastic containers fared slightly better. Also, Dr. Dimick stressed, milk stored in the dark kept its riboflavin and flavor 100 percent.

Old-Fashioned Preservative

An old-fashioned way to keep milk or cream from souring in hot weather is to stir in a small quantity of bicarbonate of soda.

BREAD AND PANCAKES

Stuffing Shortcut

Don't go through the work of pulling bread apart for stuffing or meatloaf. Put several slices on a breadboard and cut through in close small slices, lengthwise and then crosswise. You'll be done in a minute.

Fastest Way to Freshen Bread or Rolls

Sprinkle slightly stale bread with a few drops of water, wrap snugly in aluminum foil and place in a hot oven for 5 to 10 minutes or until thoroughly heated.

Most Efficient Way to Pack a Sandwich

If you're sending sandwiches for your kid's lunch at school, or brown bagging your own, try preparing several days' worth of sandwiches at the same time and freezing them. Then pack them frozen for school or work in the morning and they'll thaw out nicely by lunchtime. This will keep the sandwiches fresh-tasting and protect you from possible bacteria growth.

Painless Pancakes

Having trouble spooning? Next time you make pancakes try dipping the spoon in water or milk first. The batter will drop off the spoon quicker and more evenly.

SOUP

Best Soup

When making soup, remember the old cook's maxim: "Soup boiled is soup spoiled." It should be

cooked gently and evenly. However, slow boi[...]
fine for making stock.

Fastest Soups

Green soups. Almost any green vegetable, frozen or leftover, can be converted into a great soup in a jiffy. Start with frozen peas, broccoli, spinach or asparagus, combine with a chopped onion in a pot with 4 cups of chicken stock and simmer for 30 minutes. (If you start with already-cooked vegetables you can eliminate the simmering, but do not use the onion in that case.) Run through the blender or food processor in batches and return to pot. Add 2 cups of milk or half-and-half, salt and pepper, and heat thoroughly, but *do not boil*.

Cheapest Soup Stock

Simmer leftover bones from steaks and roasts with mushroom stems, celery tops, tomato skins or other oddments from your refrigerator. Put in a whole onion with a few cloves pinched in. Simmer for several hours. If fresh bones are used, brown them first in the oven.

Uncurdled Cream of Tomato Soup

To keep the hot milk from curdling, either thicken it first with flour and add the tomato juice just before serving, or reverse the procedure by adding thickened tomato juice to the hot milk before serving.

Fat Chance

To eliminate fat from soups, drop ice cubes into the pot. While you stir, the fat will begin to stick to the cubes. Discard them before they melt too much— or wrap cubes in a piece of cheesecloth and skim over the top of the soup.

t Soup

oo much salt in your soup, don't
grate a raw potato and add, it will
Other ways: add a teaspoon of sugar
or a few pieces of raw turnip and simmer a little
longer.

How to Get the Most Out of Canned Soup

Instead of adding a can of water, as many canned
soup manufacturers recommend, cheat! Add a can
and a half—you'll find most soups are just as good.

Food and Drink

In summer, nothing is more delicious than a cold
soup ladled from an ice bucket, which keeps it cool
for second servings.

DIPS AND SAUCES

Quick Dip

This dip goes with fresh vegetables or can be
served with ham. Mix 1 cup of mayonnaise, ¼ cup
wine vinegar, 1 teaspoon hickory smoked salt, 2
tablespoons mustard, and 1 teaspoon horseradish
sauce.

Hollandaise in a Hurry

Using a wire whisk, beat a cup of milk into a cup
of mayonnaise over low heat. When bubbly, remove
from heat and add the juice of 1 lemon.

Homemade Tomato Sauce

This takes one minute and no cooking! Use 1
pound of tomatoes (a 16-ounce can of juice may be
substituted), 2 tablespoon oil, 1 small coarsely
chopped onion, ½ cup fresh basil leaves, 1 clove
garlic, 1 teaspoon salt, and a dash of pepper. Blend

half the tomatoes and all the other ingredients at high speed. Then add the remaining tomatoes and adjust the seasonings.

FISH

Lean Tip

An economical and effective method of keeping pounds off is to eat more fish and less beef. One pound of beef has approximately 1,500 calories, whereas a pound of fish averages out at about 400 calories.

Cheapest Way to Sweeten Fish

Fish wrapped in plastic may not be "sweet" and may even be tough. A solution of a small amount of vinegar in water with a trace of salt will sweeten the flesh and restore its pungency. Place the solution in a china or well-tinned metal vessel and soak the fish in it for a few hours before cooking.

Most Efficient Way to Bake Fish

Do it by the inch. Measure the fish at its thickest point and then bake it at 350°, allowing 5 minutes for every half inch of its width.

Quickest Way to Get an Aspic

A few drops of vinegar—white or cider—in the gelatin solution will help the aspic or any other unsweetened gelatin mixture set faster.

MEAT AND POULTRY

Most Efficient Way to Buy Meat

If you have a large freezer and a versatile cook handy, consider buying a whole animal. Pound for pound, it's usually cheaper whether pig or steer.

Of course, if you have a family whose members only like hamburgers or pork chops this method is not for you: to make the purchase of a whole carcass economically sound you have to be able to utilize virtually all the cuts it provides.

Cheapest Poultry Buys

Meat markets or supermarket meat counters often place quantities of poultry parts, especially chicken, on sale as "bargains." Chicken necks and backs, for instance, can be packaged or sold separately for as little as 10¢ a pound in many areas. In fact, gourmets seek out these parts for special culinary treats. Fried duck wings, chicken wings cooked with garlic and escarole in olive oil, turkey wings, drumsticks, or necks all provide exceptional nourishment bargains.

Chicken necks and backs, boiled nearly to a pulp, make a useful broth or soup base, or stock that enriches vegetables. Lift the cooked chicken parts out of the broth with a sieve and allow to cool. The bones will fall away on touch and the remaining meat can be used in salads or casseroles.

Backs alone provide an especially wonderful meal when sautéed in vegetable oil with a clove of fresh garlic. Some cooks prefer to roll the backs in bread crumbs or corn flakes before sautéeing.

Speed-Up Cookery

When chopped meat is on sale, buy a quantity and shape it into meat balls, patties, and loaves—then freeze. Wrap each in Saran Wrap or separate with wax paper and put enough for each meal in a Baggie.

Fastest Way to Coat Meat, Poultry, and Fish for Frying

Put the meat, along with the seasoned flour or

crumbs and seasonings, into a paper bag and shake vigorously. (If your recipe calls for eggs, milk, or other liquids, use a large plastic sandwich bag.) You'll find that this method is not only quicker and less messy than other methods, but it also promotes a more even coating of the meat's surface.

Stop Splatter Easily

Cover your frying pan with an inverted collander to stop bacon or other fatty foods from splattering.

Five Tips for Meat Flavoring

Most meats can be improved by marinating. Here are some ideas for flavoring and for tenderizing less expensive cuts of meat. Overnight (or at least several hours) of marinating gives the best results.

- Soak beef stew or immerse a chuck steak in 1 cup of red wine, ½ cup of soy sauce, 2 minced cloves of garlic, 1 chopped onion, a crushed bay leaf, and a dozen peppercorns.
- Marinate beef in ½ cup oil (olive oil has an especially good flavor), the juice of 1 lemon, ½ cup whisky, and a minced glove of garlic.
- Soak lamb for stew in 1 cup of plain yogurt flavored with 2 teaspoons of curry powder. This is also good for shish kabob meat.
- Soak broiling chickens in ½ cup oil, ½ cup dry vermouth, the juice of 1 lemon, 2 minced shallots, and a pinch of thyme or rosemary.
- Pork cuts for roasting can be soaked in ½ cup of oil mixed with ½ cup of orange juice. Add a chopped onion and chopped fresh ginger.

Easy Burger Form

Use an ice cream scoop to form burgers. Simply drop the ball of meat on a griddle and press with spatula. You'll have a thick, round burger.

Cheap Frying Hash

Don't waste shortening or butter when frying canned hash. Dump it right into the fry pan (even if it isn't Teflon) and fry on a low heat. There is enough fat in the hash to fry it well, and it doesn't come out as mushy this way.

More Economy Meatloaf Tips

Add oatmeal to your meatloaf mix or try corn-meal (both are tasty stretchers). Slip a hard-boiled egg or two in the middle for flavor—the loaf will look so pretty when you slice it!

Fastest Meat Pie

Place leftover stew or pieces of leftover roast (beef, lamb, or veal) in a casserole. Add freshly cooked potatoes, onions, and carrots which have been sim-mered together, and leftover or canned gravy. Cover with mashed potatoes and bake in 350° oven for ½ hour.

Fastest Way to Tell High Quality Pork

Contrary to what your mother may have told you back when government meat inspection and live-stock-raising practices were each less efficient than they are now, and when the concern about trichi-nosis was justifiably greater, the best quality fresh pork in the stores today will have a good bright-pink color. In fact, the pinker the pork, the better. Of course, when cooked, the pork should be gray right through to the center.

Pork Economy

Instead of buying pork chops, buy pork roast. It's cheaper and you can cut it into chops yourself.

Most Efficient Turkey

The larger the turkey, the more meat per pound.

Turkey is one of those meats for which the [possibil]ities for leftovers—cold sandwiches, salads, ca[sser]oles—are almost endless. So next time you're wo[n]dering whether to buy the big one or the small one—think big.

Fastest Fat-Free Gravies

Strain the liquid from your roasting pan into a bowl—metal works fastest—and place it in the freezer for a few minutes. The fat will rise to the top and solidify and then can be removed easily.

PASTA

Best Way to Keep Your Pasta from Sticking

Add a little vegetable oil to the water before you put the pasta in.

Fastest Route to an Elegant Pasta

Keep a supply of all the usual and unusual shapes of pasta on hand for a quick and easy supper. Boiled, drained, and tossed with olive oil or butter, pasta can then be dressed with any number of fast, delicious sauces. For example:

- Lightly sauté 2 cloves of garlic in ¼ pound of butter, then add ½ pound of sliced mushrooms, 2 cups of diced ham (use leftover baked ham or sliced, boiled ham) and a bunch of chopped parsley. Heat thoroughly and add a spoonful or two of water from the boiling spaghetti if you want more liquid.
- Brown a clove of garlic in 2 tablespoons of olive oil, add a can of grated tuna fish, several chopped fresh tomatoes (you can use canned tomatoes if necessary), some chopped parsley and a sprinkle of basil or oregano. Simmer for just 2 or 3 minutes.
- Brown several medium-sized onions in a table-

oil. Add 2 anchovy fillets, minced;
s of chopped parsley; 1 pound of
bes; ½ cup dry white wine; and sea-
mmer for 30 minutes.

is delicious peasant recipe:
Boil a ch of broccoli, cut in 1-inch pieces, or a
head of cauliflower broken into pieces, along with
the pasta of your choice. Drain together. In a deep,
heavy pot, brown 2 minced cloves of garlic in ¼
cup of olive oil, add ½ teaspoon of oregano, then
add the pasta and broccoli or cauliflower to the pot
and heat through.

All these delicious dishes are even better sprinkled with fresh grated Parmesan or Romano cheese.

POTATOES

Quickest Baked Potatoes

Push skewers through the centers to distribute
the heat faster. Most hardware and houseware stores
sell fat aluminum "nails" just for the job.

How to Reuse Baked Potatoes

Leftover baked potatoes? Here's an economical
way to reheat them without burning or flavor loss:
dip the spuds in hot water and simply bake again
in a moderate oven. Or, slice them for home fries.

Give Hash Browned Potatoes a Golden Glow

Just add a teaspoon or two of vinegar to the
butter and potatoes in the skillet, and keep turning
until they're crusty brown.

Fast Home Fries

Peel an already peeled potato and let each curl
fall into a pan of shortening and fry. You'll have
the most delicious home fries ever!

Mashed Potato Secret

A well-beaten white of an egg added to mashed potatoes makes them fluffier and tastier.

Fastest Scalloped Potatoes

Arrange sliced potatoes with seasonings and cream sauce (add cheese, chives, or onions if you wish) in a buttered skillet, cover tightly and cook on top of the stove over low heat. Or save more time and use condensed mushroom or celery soup for sauce.

Ten Best Ways to Serve Potatoes

- For an entrée, scoop center from a baked potato, fill with crumbled Italian sweet sausage and top with seasoned breadcrumbs and grated cheese. Bake until browned and heated through, about 30 minutes.
- For a low-calorie treat, quarter baking potatoes, rub cut surfaces with a little oil and salt, and bake until brown in a hot oven.
- Wrap scrubbed new potatoes in foil with butter, salt, and a couple of cloves of garlic. Bake for about 45 minutes.
- For something special, top baked potatoes with sour cream and a small spoonful of caviar.
- Save potato peelings and bake in a hot oven until crisp—delicious salted and served with cocktails.
- For oven-fried potatoes, grease a cookie sheet or shallow roasting pan and rub with garlic. Cover with thinly sliced potatoes, overlapping as little as possible. Sprinkle with salt and pepper and crumbled oregano, dribble with olive oil, and bake in a hot oven until browned and crisp.
- Combine fluffy mashed potatoes with several mashed carrots or turnips for a new twist.
- Add small pieces of leftover ham and slices of onion to your scalloped potatoes recipe for an inexpensive main dish.

- Mix leftover mashed potatoes with grated cheese and an egg. Form into patties, dust with flour, and sauté in butter until browned.
- Great breakfast or supper casserole: line a baking dish with mashed potatoes, spread with puréed spinach and top with scrambled eggs.

ABOUT VEGETABLES

Best Way to Cook Vegetables

As little as possible, so that their flavor and vitamins are retained. Most vegetables—zucchini, green beans, chard, broccoli, cabbage, spinach, for example—can be balanced (plunged into boiling water for about 5 minutes), then refreshed under running cold water, and stir-fried in butter or olive oil with a dash of herbs and salt until heated through. Finely chopped garlic or shallots makes a good addition. Try slivered almonds for a gourmet treat.

Quickest Vitamin Shot

Liquid from cooked vegetables (not canned, as they have high levels of salt) makes a delicious vitamin-laced drink when mixed with tomato juice or used in soup.

VEGETABLES A TO Z

Fastest Way to Cook Asparagus and Broccoli

These vegetables cook twice as fast if you peel and split their stems. Also, this way the stems cook evenly with the heads.

Best Beans

When shopping for dried beans, buy those which are bright in color and the most uniform size. Bright color indicates freshness, while uniform size will promote even cooking.

How to Stop Cabbage Smell

If you love cabbage but detest the smell when it's cooking, place a heel of bread on top of the cabbage before you cover the pot and start cooking. The bread will absorb the odor.

Cheapest Green Food

Dandelions are an excellent cooked green, containing both vitamin A and iron. The plants are certainly abundant, and are the first edible green of the spring season. Cooked without their blossoms in vinegar they taste a bit like spinach. They are best harvested by inserting a strong knife under the "crown" of the plant and cutting at a point as far down the root as possible. Dandelions cut only at the surface of the soil will grow back in a day or so, if that is desirable.

Dandelion seed is listed in the 1980 Burpee seed catalogue on page 113 without editorial comment or planting instructions. A packet is 60¢ or you can buy a half-ounce of dandelion seed for $2.25.

Cheapest Way to Harvest Dandelion Greens

Harvesting dandelions from a lawn is a generally accepted way to exploit child labor. A supply of milk and cookies is a good idea in households that assign children to this job.

Fastest Way to Slice Mushrooms

Use an egg slicer.

Fastest Stuffed Mushrooms

Wash mushroom caps thoroughly, but do not cook. Stuff with Boursin cheese softened with sour cream. (Bake for 15 minutes if you prefer to serve them hot.)

Onions Without Tears

Slicing onions under water is the standard procedure for avoiding tears. But unless those onions are carefully dried they cause dangerous spattering if your next step is to fry them in hot fat. A simple alternative is to put the onions into the refrigerator well in advance of the time you plan to use them. Cold, like water, inhibits the stinging effect of an onion.

Most Efficient Way to Peel Onions

Peeling and cutting onions can be a difficult and even dangerous chore. The slippery inside layers of the onion are tricky to handle. The best way to get around this difficulty is to slice the onion before removing the peel. Then the outer ring of peel can be slipped off each slice with little effort and no waste.

Fastest Way to Prepare Dried Peas

Split peas for soup may be boiled without soaking. Whole peas, however, need the soaking routine. But don't despair, there is a shortcut for preparing whole peas and dried beans. Boil them for 2 minutes. Then remove from heat and let them soak for 1 hour. They will now be ready for cooking without the standard overnight soaking.

Easiest Way to Remove Water from Boiled Spinach

Press the spinach firmly between two plates.

Most Efficient Green Vegetable—Swiss Chard

Swiss chard—a close relative of spinach—may be the most useful garden vegetable in the world. It grows almost anywhere in relatively cool climates and produces all season in both hot and cool temperatures wherever grown. It is easily harvested, and bunches of it from the grocery store or produce market may be used almost "as is" except for a quick wash—unlike spinach with its sand or other green vegetables that must be shelled, trimmed, sliced, or cooked longer than 5 minutes. Its crumbled leaves are rich in vitamins A and C and iron.

Raw Swiss chard leaves have a musky richness—completely different from lettuce—that inspires its use in gourmet salads with mushrooms and bacon bits. Chef's salad with Swiss chard leaves, cheese, and meat bits is nearly a meal in itself.

Cooking Swiss chard is easy in a little water, or vinegar may be added. The white stems can be steamed like asparagus. Marinated and spiced with an herb like tarragon, Swiss chard in sour cream with raw onion is excellent with lamb.

Cooked or raw, Swiss chard may be frozen at home for later use.

Most Efficient Way to Ripen Tomatoes

The best way for tomatoes to ripen is naturally, on the vine. When this is impossible, the best way to home-ripen them is not, as is commonly believed, to put them on a sunny windowsill. Rather, the tomatoes should be put on heavy paper, leaving a space between them so that their skins are not touching, and kept in a fairly light place out of direct sunlight and at a temperature of less than 75°F. Once ripe, they should be stored, unwrapped, in the refrigerator.

Fastest Way to Peel a Tomato

Drop the tomato into boiling water for 30 seconds. Then immerse it quickly in cold water. You will be able to peel off the skin easily with your fingers.

Another method is to impale the tomato on a fork and hold over a low gas flame. Turn gently to heat evenly, then rinse with cold water and the skin comes right off.

SEASONINGS

To Use Aging Garlic

Peel the garlic cloves, cut them in half and place them in a jar of salad oil. This lengthens the life of the garlic while supplying you with a gourmet oil for salads and other uses.

How to Keep Parsley

Parsley keeps best in a plastic bag, frozen. When you need some, simply cut off some sprigs with scissors and toss the rest back in the freezer.

SALAD SHORTCUTS

Preservation Tip

Lettuce and celery keep much longer if you store in paper bags in the refrigerator instead of plastic ones.

How to Dry Lettuce

If you don't own a salad spinner, a quick way to get rid of excess water is to wrap washed greens (lettuce, endive, spinach, or whatever) in a dish towel and swing and shake vigorously until moisture stops flying out.

Cuke Alert

Almost all cucumbers that are store-bought have been dipped in paraffin wax to preserve them. Do not eat the skins!

Crispest Cole Slaw

Cut a cabbage head in half and soak in ice water for 1 hour. Then cut for cole slaw. It's the crispest ever.

Healthiest Party Food

Dishes of raw, freshly sliced vegetables—carrots, turnips, celery, cucumbers, radishes, green peppers, squash, cauliflower, even parsnips—as a cocktail party snack, perhaps with a spicy yogurt dip. Some hosts and hostesses like to be elegant and use the French word for hors d'oeuvres: it is *cruditées*, pronounced CRUH DEE TÁY.

Ten Best Salad Ideas

- Keep washed greens loosely wrapped in a clean dish towel in the refrigerator, ready to be tossed with your favorite dressing.
- Add a surprise taste to your salad . . . bits of feta or ricotta cheese, ripe olives, juice from a pickle jar, a few capers, pickled eggplant, slivers of red roasted peppers.
- A salad of sliced beets and Spanish onion rings is quick to prepare and looks as appetizing as it tastes.
- When preparing any of the following for dinner, cook a double portion: asparagus, cauliflower, carrots, broccoli, or green beans. Marinate overnight in a good oil and vinegar dressing, then serve on lettuce leaves with a sprinkling of freshly ground pepper.
- Fast and refreshing . . . a big bowl of quartered tomatoes and sliced red onions, tossed with garlic-flavored oil and vinegar. Snips of fresh basil are the perfect garnish.
- Crisp Chinese cabbage cut in rounds and topped with cottage cheese and dressing is pretty, quick, and cool.
- Marinate sliced cucumbers overnight in a sour cream dressing with fresh dill, and they'll be ready to serve at lunch or dinner.
- Cook a few extra strips of bacon at breakfast, drain well and refrigerate. At salad-making time crumble bacon over well-washed spinach and sliced

raw mushrooms. A little dry mustard added to the dressing gives a special tang.

- Use leftovers, such as pieces of ham or chicken, cold vegetables and cheese, for a hearty luncheon salad. Toss with dressing, serve on lettuce and garnish with hard-boiled eggs.
- Serve thinly sliced oranges with sweet onion rings and curly endive.

LEFTOVERS

Fastest Way to Use Leftovers of Almost Anything

Learn to make delicious, nourishing soups from leftovers in your blender or food processor. Mashed potatoes, green peas, carrots, broccoli, or asparagus blended with milk and seasoning can be heated with flour and butter for cream soups; ripe tomatoes, green peppers, cucumber, onion, and seasonings make zesty gazpacho.

Most Nutritious Leftovers

Those eaten cold. Each time food is reheated it loses some of its nutritional value (how much depends on the specific food). With foods which are best eaten hot—leftover chili, for example, or casseroles—reheat only the exact amount you plan to eat at one sitting. That way, each serving will be reheated only once and nutritional loss will be kept to a minimum.

FRUIT AND FRUIT DESSERTS

Healthiest Applesauce

Quarter apples and remove seeds *but do not* peel. Simmer with a small amount of water for 15 or 20 minutes or until soft. Put through food mill, add cinnamon and a squeeze of lemon.

Fastest Applesauce

Peel, core, and chop 2 medium apples. Put them in the blender. Add 1 teaspoon maple syrup, ¼ cup of apple juice, ½ teaspoon cinnamon, ¼ teaspoon nutmeg, and a squeeze of lemon. Blend—and you have homemade applesauce for unexpected guests.

Fastest Way to Ripen an Avocado

Place the unripened avocado in a paper bag with a ripe apple. This will speed up the ripening process. The method should work for any fruit.

Frosted Grapes

Dip small clusters of grapes into beaten egg white, shake off the excess, and dip in granulated sugar. Place on wax paper, allow 15 to 20 minutes for sugar to dry and "frost" the grapes. These look festive as part of a fruit centerpiece, and garnish for a fruit cup, or even surrounding the Christmas turkey.

Smart Way to Buy Lemons

When buying lemons, take the ones with the smoothest skin and smallest endpoints. Growers will tell you that round lemons are much superior to long ones when it comes to juice and taste.

Best Ideas for Lemons

• Substitute 1 teaspoon of fresh lemon juice for cream of tartar in a three-egg meringue.
• Make lemon flowers with shells left over from squeezing juice. (You can freeze them until ready to use.) Using kitchen shears, cut seven petals to within ½ inch of center. Round them off or trim to a point, spread them out, and with a toothpick

secure a cranberry or maraschino cherry in the center of each flower. Use to decorate salads, buffet platters, etc.

- Decorate lemon wedges served with fish with paprika, chopped parsley, ground pepper, or strips of pimento. Glamorize lemon cartwheels (unpeeled slices) by notching edges with kitchen shears or a sharp knife.
- With fish, serve half a lemon wrapped in cheesecloth tied with string or ribbon for a fine restaurant touch. Cheesecloth lets juice flow smoothly without seeds. Fresh lemon juice in cooking water keeps vegetables white while cooking—good for potatoes, cauliflower, turnips, celery, and also rice.
- Add freshly grated lemon peel to cookie recipes, frostings, puddings, and even soups for extra zest.
- Substitute lemon juice for vinegar in salad dressing.
- Squeeze half a lemon over seafood salads for a fresh, tangy flavor.
- To extract the most juice, have lemon at room temperature or heat it in hot water, and roll firmly on counter before squeezing.
- Lemons keep in the refrigerator for up to 6 weeks; at room temperature for about 10 days.

Fastest Way to Peel an Orange

Heat the orange slightly for 3 or 4 minutes before peeling—a time-saver for citrus lovers.

Fastest Way to Ripen a Persimmon

Put the persimmon in the freezer for 24 hours. When the fruit defrosts, it will be soft.

Pineapple and Strawberries St. Teresa

Wash a pint of strawberries but do not hull. Combine with 2 cups of cubed fresh pineapple and place in mounds on 4 dessert plates. Half fill a cordial

glass with orange liqueur and place next to the fru...
add 3 tablespoons of confectioner's sugar to each
plate (on a shiny green galax or lemon leaf, if you
have one). Guests pick up a piece of fruit with a
cocktail pick, dip it into the liqueur and then into
sugar.

Freezer Strawberry Jam

Purée 1 quart of ripe strawberries in a blender or
food processor, place in a bowl, and add 1 tablespoon grated orange rind and 4 cups sugar. Mix
together 2 tablespoons lemon juice and ½ bottle of
liquid fruit pectin (6-ounce size). Stir everything
together for 3 minutes, ladle into jars, and let stand
at room temperature until set, about 24 hours. Store
in freezer.

CAKES, COOKIES AND CANDY

Red and White Baking Brick

Next time you bake, add cherry Jello powder to
the eggs and milk of a white cake mix. It makes the
mix go further and adds a wonderful homemade
flavor.

Relief from a Sticky Situation

To prevent cakes from sticking, sprinkle the tins
with equal parts of flour and sugar.

Heavenly Idea

An angel food cake will slice easily without crum-
bling or sticking to the knife if you freeze it for 24
hours, then thaw.

Cake Decorating

To give a simple cake a festive appearance, cover
it with a decorative paper doily, sift confectioner's
sugar over the top, and remove the doily to reveal a
lovely, lacy pattern.

Secret

... on a homemade cake usually cracks after a
... Add a pinch of baking powder when you
mix it and it will stay moist, fresh, and tasty.

Patterned Cookies

Mix an egg yolk with ¼ cup water, divide mixture
among several cups, and add a few drops of different food colorings to each cup. Paint cookies with a
soft brush before baking.

Tips for Better Home-Baked Cookies

Preheat the oven to the recommended temperature so that the dough sets in the desired shape.
Grease cookie sheet with unsalted fat, sweet butter,
or beeswax. Fill out the cookie sheet, spacing cookies the same distance apart so that they brown
evenly. Always remove cookies from the baking
sheet promptly, so that baking process stops. Cool
cookies on a rack that allows air to circulate freely.

Improvised Baking Sheet for Cookies

Turn a flat roasting or baking pan upside down.

Nourishing Ice Cream Sodas

Sodas made at home in your blender or food processor are especially good for children. Milk or ice
cream can be whirred with bananas, fresh peaches,
strawberries, apricots, or orange juice. Try 2 cups
of orange juice with a pint of vanilla ice cream for
an Orange Cream Freeze.

Most Efficient Way to Cut Marshmallows

Avoid a sticky mess by freezing marshmallows
before cutting them.

Best Popcorn

Put popcorn in the freezer for a day or two before using and it will pop big and tender just like Orville's!

Quick and Easy Popcorn Balls

Preheat oven to 250°, place 2 quarts of popped corn in a buttered baking pan and keep warm in oven. Melt 3 tablespoons of butter over low heat, add 2 cups of colored miniature marshmallows and stir until melted. Blend in 2 tablespoons of gelatin powder, pour mixture over warm popcorn, mix well, and form into balls.

Fastest Sugar-Free Candy

If you're one of the many these days who are worried about the effects of too much refined sugar—or even if you're not—you can have terrific, easy-to-make candy without using any refined sugar at all.

Mix 1 part honey with 1 part natural peanut butter and 2 parts dry skim milk. Spread the mixture in a shallow pan and put it in the refrigerator until it chills. Cut the resulting candy into squares for serving. It's that simple. Your kids will love it and so will you.

Chapter 4
DRINK

LIQUOR

Easiest Way to Get Free Cocktail-Mixing Books

Manufacturers of cocktail ingredients, like bitters or fruit extracts, as well as liquor companies often provide free drink-mixing booklets. They may be on the counter at your liquor store or are available on request from the various companies. Most of them emphasize the manufacturer's own product, of course, but with a collection of the booklets from various sources the at-home bartender can assemble a fairly complete library of drink recipes.

Quickest Way to Chill Bottled Drinks

If refrigeration space is not available or you're in a hurry, fill a tub or other container with ice—preferably broken up or in cubes—and sprinkle with a liberal amount of salt (rock salt is ideal for this purpose). When warm bottles are tucked into the salted ice they tend to chill quickly, because the salt "wants" to melt the ice and draws heat from whatever is near it—in this case, drinks.

Cheapest Cocktail Glasses

The jars used for the 5-ounce size of Holsum Imported Spanish olives make excellent, durable cocktail glasses—just right for old-fashioneds. For those who like Spanish olives, the glasses, in effect, are free.

Most Efficient Way to Chill a Glass

Fill a glass with crushed ice; do not invert it in ice, as many bartenders do. When you invert it, the outside gets wet and drips all over your clothes.

How to Frost a Glass

Dip the glass in beaten egg white to about ¼ inch of the rim, then dip the rim in sugar. Allow to dry. Good for daiquiris.

A Twist, Please

Next time you use a lemon, scrape the rind thoroughly, place in a Baggie and freeze. Then for your next martini you'll have a rind all ready.

Summer Slices

On hot summer days, jars filled with lemon and lime wedges and orange slices, all ready for drinks, are a welcome sight in your refrigerator—and also save time.

How to Serve Drinks at a Cocktail Party

You can save liquor and avoid spots on your rug and furniture by not filling glasses to the brim. People stand up at a cocktail party and over-full glasses spill easily.

Best Blender Drinks

- To 1½ ounces of white rum add the juice of ½ lime, 1 teaspoon of sugar and ½ banana. Blend with 1 cube of cracked ice.
- Add the white of an egg to 1½ ounces of white rum, 2 tablespoons of heavy cream, and a couple of dashes of crème de cacao or Kahlua. Whir with cracked ice.

Mintiest Black Russian

1 ounce minted chocolate liqueur, ½ ounce coffee liqueur, and 1½ ounces of vodka poured over ice.

Liveliest Grasshopper

Equal parts of chocolate liqueur, green crème de menthe and heavy cream. Shake well with ice and strain.

Pinkest Spiked Lemonade

To a quart of lemonade, made from scratch or the frozen kind, add a cup of cherry liqueur, stir and pour over ice cubes in tall glasses.

Coldest Vodka

For a bottle of icy vodka, insert bottle into empty milk carton (half-gallon size), fill carton with water and freeze. Strip off carton and serve vodka straight with black bread and caviar. Very Russian!

Pinkest Vodka Drink

Add a dash of cranberry juice to the traditional

vodka and tonic for a pink tint that looks luscious with a green twist of lime.

WINE

Cheapest Way to Buy Wine

Buy wines in advance of the season when they are most popular. Buy white and rosé wines, for example, in the spring, before the summer rush is on; buy winter wines in October before the high-priced holiday season arrives.

Good Cheap Imported Wine

Although *good* and *cheap* are subjective judgements, we think all the following wines can be recommended to most people as quite drinkable. All sell for under $3 per bottle, and at that price are considerable bargains.

Premiat (Rumanian)

Cabernet sauvignon (red)	$2.49
Pinot noir (red)	$2.49
Riesling (white)	$2.49

Wines of the World(Algerian)

Dahra (red)	$1.99
Medea rouge (red)	$1.99

Folonari (Italian) (liter bottles)

Soave (white)	$2.89
Bardolino (red)	$2.89
Valpolicella (red)	$2.89

Juan Hernandez (Spanish)

Burgella (red)	$1.99

Maison Jacquin (French)

Le Royal (red)	$2.99

Vin de France (French)

L' archeveque (white)	$2.29

Most Efficient Wine Storage

The absence of bright light and vibration and a

reasonably uniform cool temperature are the essentials for good wine storage. Wine which is to be drunk in a year or two will survive in anything except direct sun. But for longer storage, darkness is essential.

A temperature of 55° to 60°F is ideal, but even if it is 10° higher, it won't ruin the wine. What will ruin it is extreme variations of temperature within short periods of time.

To minimize vibrations, keep the wine away from appliances that vibrate and be sure to store the bottles with their labels showing so they can be read without being turned.

Fastest Way to Let Wine Breathe

Using a funnel, pour your wine from bottle to decanter and back again a total of ten times. The added oxygen (the equivalent of several hours of "breathing") will mellow the wine and improve its taste.

Pinkest White Wine

To a large glass of chilled white wine add an ounce of Campari.

How to Serve Champagne

The fastest way to ruin good or even mediocre champagne is to pour it into one of those saucer-shaped champagne glasses that are a staple for every catering operation and every glassware manufacturer. What happens is that the wide surface of the bowl hastens the release of the fizzy shower of carbon dioxide bubbles. Proper champagne service requires a V-shaped flute or tulip-shaped copita; both glasses slow down the flow of bubbles by concentrating them in a tiny point at the bottom of the glass.

TEA AND JUICES

Fastest "Lift" from Coffee

You can get approximately the same amount of caffeine as there is in a cup of coffee from a tablet of caffeine citrate, costing little more than 1¢ at any drugstore. Caffeine is the only commonly used stimulant that can be bought without a prescription. At $3 a pound, a cup of black coffee costs five times as much.

Low Calorie Pepper-Uppers for Summer

Rose hip tea with an equal part of natural unsweetened apple juice is a 58-calorie energy booster.

Other high-vitamin teas:

Pink mint tea, with ⅓ cup of unsweetened grape juice and honey added to taste.

Pink lemon tea with berry juice and honey.

A mixture of equal parts of red clover tea, hibiscus tea, pear juice, and honey.

Cheapest Tea Bags

Those you use the second time. Tea bags are made to brew several cups of tea. If you only want one or two cups at the moment, set the bag aside to dry out and use it again.

Low Calorie Winter Warmup

Two cups of beef bouillon heated with 2 cups of vegetable juice and ½ teaspoon of Tabasco. Serve in mugs with lime slices.

Most Satisfactory Cocktail Substitute

Nonalcoholic drinks can be spiced up with a few drops of bitters. Or add Bloody Mary mix to a glass of tomato juice. Or mix fruit juice in standard selt-

zer water. Dry ginger ale can also be used as a
base.

Freshest-Tasting Orange Juice

If you don't have any time to squeeze from scratch,
add the juice of one orange or one lemon to the
juice from a container or to the juice you make
from a can of frozen concentrate.

Chapter 5
HOUSE

KITCHEN TIPS

Cheapest Handy-Wipes

Slightly used paper napkins. Tossed in a basket on the kitchen counter, dinner napkins can be used to wipe up spills, muddy prints, or to clean out a greasy pan before washing.

Cheapest Aluminum Foil

The foil you use for the second and third time. Most aluminum foil can be wiped off, stored, and used again. Remember, aluminum is not a renewable resource!

S-t-r-e-t-c-h Your Plastic Stretch Wrap

Usually, plastic wrap can be reused. Set it aside to dry, or wipe it carefully, then wrap it around an empty roller you have saved for just this purpose.

Free Cardboard Cartons

From the nearest liquor store, if someone hasn't beaten you to it.

Cheese It!

Cheese comes off the grater easily if you lightly wipe the grater beforehand with cooking oil.

Best Way to Clean a Grater

A vegetable brush is better than a dishrag in cleaning a vegetable grater. It not only permits a more thorough job, it doesn't snag.

Most Efficient Way to Clean a Knife

When cleaning steel knives, add a bit of bicarbonate of soda to the cleaning powder to help remove stains.

Easy Oven Cleaning

When food explodes in an oven, an ammonia-soaked cloth can be helpful. Place on the burned spots for an hour and you will then be able to scrape off the spots without damaging the stove's enamel.

Cheapest Way to Keep Your Garbage Disposal Fresh

Use citrus peels. Save them in a covered container in your refrigerator, and grind a bit in the garbage disposal each day. They'll keep it smelling fresh and pleasant.

KITCHEN
ENERGY-SAVING APPLIANCES

Fastest Way to Check the Seal on Your Refrigerator Door

Loose or inadequate seals on the refrigerator door could be costing you money. The quickest way to find out is to stick an ordinary piece of writing paper in the door. If the paper can be pulled out of the closed door without effort, the seal is too loose and you could probably save money by repairing or replacing it.

How to Reduce Refrigerator Operating Costs

Keep condenser coils (at back or bottom of refrigerator) clean. Keep freezer compartment packed full; if necessary, fill empty spaces with bags of ice cubes, or fill milk cartons with water and freeze.

Most Efficient Refrigerator

Refrigerators and freezers with manual defrost use considerably less energy than those with an automatic defrost feature. You may find the savings on your electricity bill worth the extra effort it takes to defrost your refrigerator manually.

If you do have a manual defrost refrigerator or freezer, be sure to defrost it regularly, or whenever frost builds up to a thickness of ¼ inch. Any greater buildup of frost increases the unit's energy use.

Most Efficient Refrigerator Location

Plan your kitchen so that the refrigerator is in the coolest part of the room, as far from the stove and oven as possible.

Most Efficient Freezer Temperature

For the most effective and economical freezer operation, the Association of Food and Drug Officials recommends a temperature of 0°F (-17.8°C). The inside of your refrigerator should be kept between 37°F and 40°F (2.8°C and 4.4°C).

Most Efficient Storage Freezers

Department of Energy tests indicate that chest freezers are 18 percent less expensive to run than upright models. An upright freezer lets the cold air spill out, while chest freezers, whose hinged lids open upward, tend to retain the air. However, the cost difference may also be affected by the way in which the two freezer types tend to be used. Uprights, which take less space, are frequently in main traffic centers. Chests are in garages or utility rooms and likely to be opened less often.

How to Save Energy when Cooking

Turn off burner two or three minutes before end of cooking time—heat retained in the burner and in the pot will finish the cooking process. Turn off the oven 5 to 10 minutes ahead of time. A hot oven will still maintain its heat for at least 10 minutes after you turn it off. In this way you'll save approximately one-sixth of your cooking fuel bill for every hour of cooking.

Use tight-fitting covers on pots and pans to retain heat and speed cooking.

Use pots which fit the size of burners, and use lowest possible heat setting to cook foods on the top of the stove. Plan meals to utilize the oven to its fullest—cook as many items in the oven at one time as possible. Don't preheat the oven unless absolutely necessary.

Have a wood stove? Keep a kettle of water on top and use hot water in it to start vegetables on stove or to make a cup of tea. And the top of the wood stove is a good place to keep foods warm—for free!

Check the housewares department for an insert which will enable you to cook two or three vegetables in the same pot.

Most Efficient Ignition for a Gas Stove

A modern electronic ignition can save 50 percent of the gas required by a gas stove compared to the old pilot light system.

Cheapest Way to Dry Dishes

If your dishwasher lacks one of the new "Energy Saver" buttons, the best way to save energy is not to use the dry cycle. Let your dishes drip-dry. Open the door of the dishwasher, allowing the circulating air to reach them. You can speed up the process even further by pulling the dish racks out.

Most Efficient Water Temperature for Garbage Disposals

Cold. Using cold water for your garbage disposal rather than hot is not only energy efficient, saving you money on your water-heating bills, it helps solidify the grease that tends to collect in such units, making it possible for the machine to grind it up and wash it away.

BATHROOM CLEANING

Most Efficient Way to Clean a Bathroom

The key to the easy and efficient maintenance of a clean bathroom, free of dirt and scum, is to clean regularly all bathroom surfaces just after a long, hot shower. You'll find that the shower has done half the work for you, virtually steam cleaning your bathroom. All you need to do is wipe off the various surfaces with a soft cloth, or, in the case of tiles or crevices, a brush.

Fastest Way to Clean the Bathtub

The surface of a porcelain bathtub usually becomes more difficult to clean and less shiny the more abrasive cleaner you use. Use warm soapy water, or plain washing soda. If you have a buildup of soap, a cloth soaked in kerosene will do the job.

Fastest Way to Remove Stains from Porcelain Sink or Tub

Cover the stain with a small rag, saturate the rag with chlorine bleach, and leave in place overnight. By morning the stain should have disappeared.

Quickest Way to Get a Room to Smell Lovely

The quickest way to add a pleasing fragrance to your room (and it's even cheaper than those room deodorants) is to drop a bit of perfume on a lit light bulb. Florals such as rose and gardenia are best.

BATHROOM
ENERGY SAVING

Best Way to Save Energy in Your Shower

Install an energy-saving flow-regulator on your showerhead. Such restrictors hold the flow of water to about 3 or 4 gallons a minute. Depending on your shower, this could cut the hot water you use in taking a shower by as much as half—a large saving in water-heating costs.

Most Efficient Toilet

While the wash-down type of toilet is generally the cheapest, the siphon-jet toilet is the most efficient.

LAUNDRY ROOM

Easiest Way to Sort Socks

Tired of sorting socks for the males in your family? Ask each member to wear a different color, or at least a different shade. It will make pairing easier and prevent arguments.

If they wear athletic socks, ask each one to choose a different color stripe.

Sweetest-Smelling Laundry

A few drops of cologne, rosewater, or orange water in the final rinse will make your laundry smell sweet. And in the summer, nothing beats drying your laundry in the fresh air.

Fastest Way to Identify Single, Double and Queen-Sized Sheets

Mark each sheet on the bottom hem with a different color darning or embroidery cotton, the brighter the better.

LAUNDRY ROOM
ENERGY SAVING

Most Efficient Washer Load Size

Always use full loads in your washing machine, unless it is specifically designed for variable loads. Never wash only a few items at a time. Running a washer with less than a full load wastes water and energy. Take care, however, not to overload, as this can cut down on the machine's cleaning effectiveness.

Most Economical Amount of Laundry Detergent

Follow the directions on the box. If your clothes are only lightly soiled you can experiment with as much as one-quarter less. The detergent companies want their products to perform as well as possible, so their instructions are reliable. Using more detergent than recommended is wasteful—of more than detergent. Too much detergent makes a machine work harder and use more energy.

Energy Saving in the Laundry

Cold water rinse. Many new machines have only cold water rinse available; new detergents rinse out completely in cold water.

Cheapest Clothes Dryer

The sun. For anyone who lives in a suitable climate, and has the time and space, the sun and a clothesline still make the cheapest and most energy-efficient clothes-drying system in the world.

Cheapest Load for Your Dryer

If you have more than one load of laundry to dry, you may be able to do your last load all but free. Save your lightweight, fast-drying items until last. With the dryer already heated up from earlier loads, you may be able to dry these items with the heat source turned off.

Most Effective Clothes Drying

Clean the lint screen after each load. A clean lint screen allows the air to flow freely through your dryer, using less energy and drying your clothes faster.

Most Efficient Use of Your Clothes Dryer

Establish your washing schedule so that your dryer will be in constant use. If necessary, do all your laundry loads first so that you will have a steady supply of clothes for your dryer. If your dryer cools off between loads, a significant amount of energy will be required to heat it up again, resulting in longer drying times and greater waste.

Most Efficient Clothes Drying

Remove bath and face towels from the dryer while still quite damp and throw them over shower rods to finish drying. Besides saving energy, the moisture is good for the house in winter.

If you are going to dry permanent press items in your dryer, use the normal spin on the washer rather than permanent press. This removes more water during spin, thus shortening the drying time. And the dryer will remove any wrinkles which might result from the normal spin.

How to Unplug Holes in Steam Iron

Poke white deposit from holes with a long needle, then flush iron with a mild solution of white vinegar and water by pouring liquid in water hole, plugging in iron, and letting it vaporize through clean ports.

How to Smooth Small Scratches from Surface of Electric Iron

Even very small scratches can slow down ironing or damage fine fabrics. Rub sole of iron with crumpled brown paper and dampened table salt, or use 4/0 (very finest) steel wool.

Most Efficient Ironing

Save your items to be ironed until there are a lot of them. Each time you iron, it takes time and energy to heat up your iron. Do them all at once and you'll save.

Fastest Way to Dampen Clothes for Ironing

For those special napkins and tablecloths, shirts and blouses, put them into a plastic bag, pour in one-fourth or one-half cup of water, depending on number of items, shake closed bag vigorously, and leave overnight. In the morning everything will be evenly damp.

Fastest Way to Iron a Large Linen Tablecloth

Pad a table thoroughly with felt or several blankets, then cover with a sheet. Keep unironed portion of your cloth wrapped in a damp towel to prevent drying out.

Best Way to Iron Embroidered Linens

Place the embroidered part of your linen cloth, mat, or napkin over a turkish towel *upside down* and press firmly until the monogram or pattern has a raised effect.

HEATING AND COOLING IN GENERAL

Most Efficient Thermostat Settings

The Department of Energy recommends that you set your thermostat at 78°F when using your air conditioner. The experts regard this as the best summertime compromise between comfort and the need to save energy—not to mention the need to save money on utility bills.

When using your furnace in the wintertime, set your thermostat at 65°F in the daytime and early evening and 55°F at night. Warning: these temperatures are unwise if there are elderly people in the house. Then the temperature should be maintained between 68°F and 70°F to reduce the risk of hypothermia.

Most Efficient Location for a Thermostat

The thermostat controls for a furnace or air conditioner should be centrally located in the house and well removed from all windows, lamps, TV sets, or other appliances. Cold air or sunlight from a window, or the heat generated by a lamp or appliance, will prevent the thermostat from accurately measuring the general temperature of the house.

Fast Cost-Cutters

You can keep both your heat and your cool by closing off unoccupied rooms and shutting off their heating or air-conditioning vents (except if you have a heat pump system which could be harmed by shutting vents).

Your kitchen, bath, or other ventilating fans should be worked only when absolutely necessary. In one hour, a fan can blow away a houseful of expensively heated or cooled air.

Fastest Way to Tell if Your Windows Need Caulking

Keeping your windows airtight can save you money on heating or air-conditioning bills. To tell if your windows would benefit from caulking or other weatherization, move a lighted candle along the frames of your windows. If the flame flickers, there's a gap between the window and the frame, and that gap is costing you money—and energy.

Cheapest Weatherization for Low-Income Families

The federal government's Weatherization Assistance program can provide low-income families with up to $800 worth of installed weatherization materials, $100 worth of energy-saving repairs to their residences and/or $50 worth of furnace repairs. In order to qualify, a family must have an income of no more than 125 percent of the poverty level established by the Office of Management and Budget. This level varies according to family size. For a family of four, for example, it's $8,375 a year. For further information, check with your state energy office or any local branch of the Office of Economic Opportunity.

Most Energy-Efficient Window Locations

In designing or buying a home in a warm climate, try to see that most of the windows are located on the north and east sides of the house, which get the least sun. This will cut down on excessive heat and save you money on air conditioning. In cold climates windows should be located on the south and west, where the greatest solar heat gain is available in the wintertime.

Most Efficient Use of Shade Trees

Deciduous trees planted on the south and west sides of your house can be a help all year round. They'll provide shade in the hot months, beauty in the fall and let the sunshine through to provide heat in the winter.

HEATING

Most Efficient Oil Furnace Modification

Simply reducing the nozzle size of your oil-burning furnace can make a substantial reduction in the size of your heating bills. A recent study found that 97 percent of the oil furnaces tested were oversized, and therefore burned more oil than was necessary to heat the house.

Fastest Way to Check the Efficiency of an Oil Furnace

Have your service man check the level of carbon dioxide in the flue of your oil-burning furnace. In general, the higher the level of carbon dioxide, the more efficient the burner. If your flue contains less than 9 percent carbon dioxide, it probably needs fixing, if not replacement.

Cheapest Energy-Saving for Your Furnace

Clean the air filter of your oil-burning furnace regularly, at least once a month during the heating season, and even more often if the furnace is located near a clothes dryer, home workshop, or other source of excessive dust and dirt in the air. The air filter on your gas furnace should be cleaned or replaced, depending on the type of filter you have, at least as often. A dirty filter restricts the air circulation in the furnace, making it work harder and less efficiently.

Cheapest Way to Keep Your Radiators Radiating

Clean radiator surfaces often. Dust and grime hamper the flow of heat. Another heat booster is to paint your radiators with a flat paint, preferrably black. Flat paint radiates heat better than glossy.

Most Efficient Draperies

Your draperies can help you save energy. Tacked at the sides and bottom, they make excellent window insulators. Take care, though, because loose draperies, open at the sides and with a space at the bottom, can actually initiate a current which will scoop air up behind them, cool the air against the cold surface of the window and send it back out into the room, making the room harder rather than easier to heat.

Cheapest Home-Heating Aid

Water. Dry air feels cooler, moist air warmer at the same temperature. A well-humidified home will feel as comfortably warm at 65°F as a dry one at over 70°F.

If you don't want to spring for a commercial dehumidifier—an energy user itself—pans of water placed near heating outlets will do much the same job for practically nothing. Also, sponges in dishes of water in cupboards and cabinets, and plants, lots of them, throughout the house.

Cheapest Distilled Water

The water gathered by your dehumidifier. Since it is free of chlorination or fluoridation, it is good for steam irons, houseplants—and car batteries.

To Reduce Drafts

- Hang a heavy drapery or bedspread over inner vestibule doorway.
- If you don't have a vestibule, consider building one. Constructed of glass, it could be a small greenhouse at your front door.
- Sew rings to ready-made quilts, hang on rods for insulating draperies over glass doors and windows.
- Panels of 2-inch styrofoam can be cut to window size, covered with fabric, and hung as interior shutters. Or simply put them in place at night, take them down during the day. Just be sure to get a tight fit.

Cheapest Way to Heat a Cool Room

If you have a too-cool room that your main heating system doesn't reach, use a kerosene space heater. New kerosene heaters are clean, effective, cheap, and *safe.*

Most Energy-Efficient Floor Plan

A square floor plan can usually be heated more efficiently than a comparable rectangular one, according to the Department of Energy. That's something to keep in mind if you're planning to build a new house.

Most Efficient Use of Fireplace

There has been much talk of the pros and cons of using a fireplace in these energy-conscious times. The number to remember is twenty. If it is 20° or more outdoors, a fire will add warmth to the room. The further the temperature goes below 20°, the greater the heat loss.

Since some of the warm air of your house is being drawn up the chimney, other energy-saving measures include lowering the thermostat (so the furnace won't have to use as much fuel to keep replacing the heat in other rooms), and installing glass doors for the fireplace to cut down on the amount of hot air that's lost.

How to Unstick Fireplace Damper

Use a long-handled brush to scrape off rust and soot, opening and closing damper until it works easily.

Cheapest Way to Keep Your Fireplace from Costing you Heating Dollars

Make sure that the damper in your fireplace is closed whenever the fireplace is not in use. This will prevent a great deal of valuable heat from your furnace being swept up the chimney. (An open damper in a 48-inch-square fireplace can cause the loss of up to 8 percent of your heat).

Cheapest Log Carrier

The one you make yourself. Any sturdy material— a remnant of pile fabric, a piece of canvas, or a length of upholstery material—can be turned into a handy log carrier. Simply cut a piece approximately 4½ feet long by 2 feet wide, notch out handles about 10 inches long, and you have a carrier that will take five or six logs.

COOLING

Cheapest Way to Cool a House

Natural ventilation. Learn to take advantage of every breeze.

Air moves in straight lines. Windows or doors must be opened across from each other to give much ventilation. (Opening a window at top and bottom does not give any more ventilation than one opening.)

Any obstruction across an opening cuts down the speed of the breeze. Even screening reduces it by 50 percent.

Breezes usually fall at sunset, so that's when you may need a fan.

Remember that the living area of a room is the six feet up from the floor. Windows above your head do little to cool you off.

Consider louvered doors and windows where you need privacy but could use a breeze.

Most Efficient Air-Cooling Device

The attic fan or "whole-house ventilating fan" sucks air into the house through the doors and windows and releases it through the attic. It is very effective in temperatures ranging into the mid-80's F, and a definite improvement on simple window fans even at temperatures above that. And an attic fan uses only about one-tenth the energy of a refrigerated air conditioner.

Cheapest Way to Cool Your House in the Summertime

Open the windows. It may seem obvious, but many of us with air conditioners often forget. In most parts of the country, open windows are all that's necessary for comfort on summer days. One of the greatest wastes of energy in many households is the tendency to turn on the air conditioner on the first hot day of summer and then leave it on till autumn.

Most Efficient Start-up Temperature for Your Air Conditioner

When turning on your air conditioner, the best temperature at which to set your thermostat is the temperature you want your house to be. Many people believe that if they set the thermostatic control extremely low when they turn their air conditioner on, the unit will cool the air faster. It won't. All it will do is cool the air below the temperature you want it to be, and waste energy doing it.

Most Efficient Air Conditioner Fan Speed

High. This speed provides better cooling. In extremely humid weather, however, a low fan speed setting will remove more humidity from the air.

Cheapest Air Conditioning

By and large, window air conditioners, wisely placed, will cost less to cool your rooms in a moderate climate than a central air-conditioning unit would.

LIGHT

Most Efficient Lighting

The fluorescent light lasts seven to ten times longer than the incandescent and is four times as efficient with its ratio of 30 percent light to 70 percent heat. The incadescent provides only 5 percent light.

Most Energy-Efficient Bulb for Directional Lamps

Reflector floodlights are about twice as efficient at producing usable light as their ordinary counterparts. While they are unsuitable for general lighting purposes, they make excellent substitutes for conventional bulbs in such fixtures as spot or pole lamps.

How to Reduce Lighting Costs

Use one large bulb rather than two or more smaller ones. One 100-watt incandescent bulb produces more light than two 60-watt bulbs, yet uses 20 percent less energy.

Save energy and trim the size of your electric bill too! When light bulbs are destined to go inside wall or ceiling fixtures, choose unfrosted bulbs. You'll find that you can reduce the wattage and increase light. The fixture itself prevents glare and softens the lighting from the clear bulb. Get more light— from lower-watt bulbs.

Most Efficient Light Switch

The solid-state dimmer light switches currently available allow you to regulate precisely the amount of light given off by your lamps. That way you use only the amount of light and energy you need at any one time.

Most Energy-Efficient Room Decor

Use a light touch. Since light colors reflect light, they cut down on the amount of artificial illumination needed, which would qualify white-on-white as the ultimate in low cost decoration.

WATER

Fastest Way to Find the Cause of Dampness

If you're troubled with too much moisture in your basement and can't tell whether it's being caused by seepage or condensation, there's a simple way to find out. Just attach a small mirror about halfway up a damp basement wall. Leave it for twenty-four hours. If after that time the mirror's surface is covered with moisture, your problem is condensation.

Fastest Way to Cure Condensation in Your Basement

Ventilate. Most condensation problems in basements are caused by inadequate ventilation. Often the fastest, cheapest, and most efficient way to solve the problem is simply to open a window.

Most Efficient Way to Waterproof Your Basement

If you have a serious leaking or seepage problem in your basement, you should remember that the most efficient place to apply your waterproofing is outside, not inside, the basement. Most waterproofing techniques for the outside are more expensive than those for the inside, but they are also much more effective.

PESTS AND RODENTS

Most Efficient Mice Control

Keep them out of your home in the first place. Killing rodents in the home is both inefficient and ineffective. In the long term, the best way to combat an infestation of mice is to make certain that the openings through which they enter the house are closed off. Any opening to your home over ¼ inch in diameter should be closed or screened off. Any possible entry areas—under doors, basement windows, etc.—which are made of gnawable materials should be covered with hardware cloth or some other, nongnawable material.

Fastest Way to Catch a Mouse

Bait the trap with peanut butter. Mice find it irresistible.

Fastest Way to Get Rid of Rats

Shut off their water. Unlike mice, rats need water every day and they won't stay anywhere where they can't get it. If a building has rats, it's virtually certain that they've found a source of water there. The fastest and safest way to get rid of them is to find that source and remove it. It could be a leaking pipe, excessive condensation, even a pet's water dish. Whatever it is, once it's gone, the rats will be too.

PHONE AND MAIL

Fastest Way to Make Overseas Telephone Calls

Many American cities now have direct dialing for overseas calls. Details are available in the front pages of telephone directories or from telephone companies. It is usually necessary to dial several digits followed by numbered codes for the country, the area code, and the actual number. In some European cities it is also possible to call the United States by dialing direct. In both cases rates are usually lower than those for operator-assisted calls.

Best Way to be Unlisted

There's no need to pay extra for an unlisted phone. Arrange for the phone to be listed under a fictitious name and tell only the people you want to talk to. Ma Bell won't care as long as she has the correct name to bill.

Fastest Cure for Obscene Telephone Calls

Screaming at an obscene caller may be just the turn-on he's looking for. Instead, use a whistle. One no-nonsense blast will pierce through even the sickest mind.

Most Efficient Way of Learning How You got on a Junk Mailing List

Use a slightly different spelling for your name, street address, or town each time you subscribe to a magazine or send away for a mail-order item. Keep a record of the different spellings and when unwanted mail is received, check your home address against the list. You will then be able to complain to the company that sold your name.

Fastest Way to Stop Receiving Junk Mail

Write to the Direct Mail Marketing Association, 6 East 43 Street, New York, New York 10017. Also write to them if you want to *start* receiving junk mail.

If you want to stop receiving unsolicited mail that you consider obscene or sexually suggestive, contact the Post Office, which has a special list of people *not* to be sent this material that all mailers of X-rated material must have.

Scratch Paper is as Close as Your Mailbox

People on insurance company mailing lists (also charity and fund drive appeals) generally have a free and continuing supply of "scratch pads," if you're willing to scribble on the unused backs of material you receive. Envelopes can also be used, slit open for you to write on their insides.

This is merely a refinement of the good old days, when school kids used brown paper bags from the local grocer before neatly copying the final work into their notebooks.

CAR

Best Octane Rating

The Department of Transportation reports that many drivers are overpaying on gas by buying a higher octane rating than they need. Check for the recommended octane rating in your car owner's manual and then check the octane rating on the gas pump. There is no advantage to upgrading.

If you can't find the owner's manual, there is a way to determine the proper octane on your own. If your engine is not knocking, try the next lower rating. Repeat this until you discover the lowest rating on which your car will run smoothly. That's your magic octane number.

Traveling Dynamite

A single gallon of gasoline stored in the trunk of a car has the explosive power of fourteen sticks of dynamite, according to the federal Consumer Product Safety Commission.

Keep it in the tank where it belongs.

Most Efficient Fuel Use

If you find yourself caught in a traffic jam or in a slow-moving line-up for a drive-in teller or in any other situation where you're likely to be at a standstill for longer than a minute, turn off your car's engine. According to the Department of Energy, it will take less energy to start it up again than it would to let it idle.

When Air Can Add Mileage

The money it takes to buy a good gauge so you can check air pressure in tires yourself will be returned within months. Using a tire below the pressure recommended in the owner's manual can lose a mile or more on a gallon of gas, and it can halve the mileage life on the tire itself.

Most Efficient Tires for Passenger Cars

Radial tires are far and away the most efficient of the commonly available types of passenger car tires. According to the U.S. Department of Energy, radials will increase a car's mileage 3 to 7 percent in ordinary driving and up to 10 percent at the 55 mph recommended highway speed, once they've been thoroughly warmed up. Quite apart from their mileage advantage, radials will last longer than other tires. It is important, however, not to mix radials with conventional tires, since such mixing is dangerous.

First Aid for the Nonstarting Car

If the car doesn't start, a pair of jumper cables and a friendly neighbor—or a passing motorist—may be all that's needed to get the battery working. Check before you phone a tow truck. It may be only that the battery needs recharging—or battery cables need cleaning and tightening.

Similarly, don't buy a new battery until you've had the old one recharged at a service station and the terminals cleaned. At the same time, make sure the alternator is checked out and working. The old battery is dead when it says so, not when someone trying to sell you a battery says so.

Fastest Line on Auto Problems

If your car's brakes are always wearing down or you're having a hard time getting your dealer to make a warranty-covered repair, the National Highway Safety Traffic Administration's toll-free hotline (800-424-9393) may be able to help you with your problem. Hotline operators will tell you, for example, whether your car's defect can be fixed or whether you're stuck with it because it's an inherent problem in the make and model.

If your major problem is getting the dealer or manufacturer to tackle your car's problem, the agency's staff will try to get cooperation for you, although they can't guarantee results.

The hotline is a valuable contact for prospective car buyers, too. Although they won't give you advice on the best or safest car to buy, the operators will tell you whether the car you're considering has any record of recalls or defects that could prove troublesome for you later on.

How to Have a Car Most Cheaply

Leasing a car for three years is cheaper than buying one and selling or trading it in. Added to the initial cost of the car are the expenses of registration fees, car insurance, and bank loan interest if part of the cost is financed. And after three years, the car will have a low resale value. On a $6,000 car the difference between owning and leasing would be several hundred dollars. In addition, leasing is less hectic. At the end of three years you can simply walk away from it, worry-free.

Cheapest Car Rental

Car rental agencies that offer subcompacts and unlimited mileage give you a head start on an economical car rental. Gas is generally not included in the package but this too saves you money if you buy the cheapest gas you can find and return the car with a full tank. Most rental agencies refill the gas tank at high rates and add this cost to the bill.

HOME SAFETY

House I.D.

The fire department may have no trouble finding your place, in the event they are called to it because of fire, but it may not be so easy for police or even a deliveryman. The number of your house should be clearly visible from the street, day or night. It could be a welcome sign indeed.

Smoke Can Kill . . . Faster!

Carbon monoxide, smoke, and lack of oxygen are overwhelmingly responsible for deaths in fires, not flames. A National Science Foundation test found that it took seven minutes for a bedroom and everything in it to be fully ablaze—but only five minutes for the toxic fumes of that blaze to destroy life.

An early warning smoke detector is considered essential in every home and, in fact, Federal Housing Administration loans on new housing actually dictate their installation.

In addition to such an early warning system, the National Fire Protection Association recommends such home safety devices as closing bedroom doors tightly at night; having and practicing escape plans; inspecting electric wiring, appliances, stoves, and heaters; not smoking in bed or when judgment is impaired by fatigue, alcohol, or medicine; and never leaving children alone in the house.

In event of a fire, the first thing to do is get everybody out of the building, and be sure no one tries to get back in. After that, call the fire department.

Be Prepared for an Emergency

Emergencies are not uncommon, and reasonable home precautions against them include such supplies as candles, canned goods (and a good old-fashioned, hand-operated can opener), a flashlight with replacement batteries, a first-aid kit, a transistor radio.

Also, keep a phone list with all the numbers you need to know taped inside the medicine cabinet and next to your phone.

Driver's License Can Identify More Than You

Most of us use our driving licenses as identification when cashing checks, taking out library cards, etc. You can also use the number on your driver's license as a helpful form of identification by etching it onto personal property like radio and television sets, bicycles, and other burglar-desirable items.

Property marked this way is less valuable to a burglar because it is self-evident proof that it has been stolen. Equally important is the fact that if it is recovered by the police it can be returned to you. Tools for etching onto wood, plastic, and metal may be borrowed from the police in some areas, or rented from hardware stores.

Don't Stash Cash

Many people keep sums of money in larger or smaller amounts stashed away at home for emergency use. It's smarter to use traveler's checks for this purpose. They're good anywhere, you don't have to be traveling to use them, and if they're stolen they're replaceable. Cash isn't.

Cheapest Way to Get a Safe-Keeping Place for Your Valuables

Detach a section of baseboard and make a hiding hole between studs. Replace baseboard using cabinet fasteners such as magnet snaps or ordinary friction snaps—or simply nail board lightly in place.

Even If You've Got It, Don't Flaunt It!

Picture windows may be great to look out of, but the view from outside in should not be too revealing. Works of art or other valuables on public display are a tempting invitation to crime.

Don't Tell the Thief What to Expect

An antitheft alarm system installed in a car (a home, an office) usually comes with a sticker announcing the fact, which is supposed to be placed in a window as a warning. It also serves as an invitation—to any thief who knows how to disconnect the advertised alarm system—and most professional thieves do.

Keeping your alarm system a secret may be a lot better than advertising it.

Your Gun Can Hurt You

The traditional explanation for a gun in the house—that it is a protection against burglars—doesn't make sense, as every police department in the country knows. If there must be a gun around, it not only should be kept unloaded but should be hidden somewhere difficult to find—and even more difficult to get at in a hurry. This holds true whether there are children in the house or not—a gun is something a burglar might find even more handy than a television set, and you might be the victim if you catch him in the act.

STAINS AND CLEANING

Getting Rid of the Worst Stains

Ballpoint pen ink: To remove from washables and nonwashables, put an absorbent towel over the stain and blot from the reverse side with glycerine. Then blot again with a second absorbent cloth or towel bearing down with a lot of pressure. For a strong fabric, rub with a toothbrush. To wash out the glycerine use a few drops of ammonia, rubbed in, then rinse with clear water. (Washing in buttermilk is also sometimes effective, but it takes a lot of rubbing, which could be dangerous to some fabrics.)

Meat or bread boards: Rub thoroughly with insides of lemon rinds, then wash with clear water. The boards will bleach white.

Perspiration: Sponge spot with white vinegar and wipe dry with clean cloth.

Dishes: If your dishes are stained brown from baking, remove stains by soaking in strong Borax and water.

Carpet: Mix Polident as you would for dentures, then brush into the stain. It will disappear and not harm your rug!

Rust: Table salt and cream of tartar will remove rust stains on a garment. Wet the spot, spread the mix on thickly, then place the garment in the sun for a while. Later, brush out.

Pitch or tar: Some believe these are "impossibles," but if you know the trick, it's simple! Just cover stains with butter, then wash thoroughly in turpentine. A good drycleaning soap used with the turpentine will help.

Hotplate: The stains left on wood table or cabinet surfaces by hotplates or hot dishes can be easily removed by applying spirits of camphor with a soft cloth (bought in any drugstore). Rub lightly and, when stain disappears, polish with soft duster.

Axle-grease: Soften with lard, then soak in turpentine. Take a knife and very carefully scrape off all the loose surface dirt. Then sponge clean with more turpentine and rub gently until dry.

Blood: If fresh, use ice water. If hard and dry, steep a few hours in cold water to which you've added a pinch of baking soda. Washing and bleaching will finish the process. Never, *ever* put blood stains in hot water!

Tea or coffee: Glycerine gently rubbed on the stain should do the trick. If the stain is old, soak in the glycerine for a few hours.

Fruit: When still moist, cover with powdered cornstarch. When dry, rinse the article in cold water and wash in the ordinary way. You may also use Borax. Rub, then hold material and pour hot water through.

Grass: Cold water and no soap. Alcohol can be used if the material is unwashable.

Chewing gum: To remove this pesky stuff, try rubbing it with ice. It should roll off and leave no marks. If it is more stubborn, rub with turpentine. Another method is to soften the gum with egg white, then scrub.

Paint from glass: You can remove paint from glass with a single-edge razor blade, but it often scratches the glass so try hot vinegar on a rag—and rub.

Aquarium high-water mark: A tiny bit of vinegar

on a rag will remove that unsightly white line that forms where the water line was in a fish tank.

Candle wax from a table: Place brown paper or paper towel over drippings and press with a warm iron, moving paper until all wax is absorbed. Or apply ice until wax is brittle and can be carefully lifted with a knife.

Wax buildup from furniture: Rub surface evenly and lightly with a soft cloth dipped in paint thinner.

Water spots from wood furniture or floors: Rub ring or spot with petroleum jelly, leave overnight. If spot hasn't disappeared, repeat the application.

Cigarette stains from a marble surface: Make a paste of hydrogen peroxide and talcum powder, rub on stained area, then add a drop or two of ammonia. After a few minutes wash off and polish with a soft cloth.

Brick: Wash brick with warm water and trisodium phosphate (1 ounce of trisodium per gallon). Remove stubborn stains by first wetting the brick and then rubbing the surface with another piece of brick of the same color.

Mildew Treatment for Fabrics, Leather, and Furniture

If the object is portable, your first step is to take it outdoors and brush off the mildew to prevent the spores from scattering through the house. Larger items should be vacuumed and the bag thrown away. If the bag is not disposable, empty it (and clean the brush) outside if possible.

Now make a solution of half rubbing alcohol and half water. This inexpensive mixture, applied with a moistened but not soaked cloth, is an effective mildew treatment for leather, draperies, upholstered furniture, and mattresses. It may even serve to brighten faded colors. But you must be sure to test each item first for colorfastness.

Should mildew stains on colorfast clothes not come out in the wash, treat them with a mixture of lemon juice and salt, spread them in the sun, and then rinse thoroughly.

For rugs and carpets, thick suds of a mild detergent are a low-cost mildew remover. Wipe the suds away with a damp cloth and then dry the rugs as quickly as possible.

Film from Inside a Crystal Decanter

Make a solution of 1 quart of water and 2 tablespoons of vinegar, pour into decanter and let stand for 1 hour. Rinse thoroughly. If film is not removed, make a solution of fine sand and water and shake vigorously, then rinse.

Old Gold Leaf Frame

Apply a small amount of paste wax with a small, soft paintbrush, then polish very gently with a soft cloth. Do not try to remove old patina—it adds to the value and beauty of the frame.

Scratches in Furniture

Use liquid shoe polish in bottle with felt-tip applicator, or remove top and use a small paintbrush. Iodine diluted with denatured alcohol is also a good cover-up.

Reviving Old Records

The best way to enjoy old records is without surface hiss or scratching or even dirt in the grooves. To get better reproduction from your old 78 rpms and those 45's and 33⅓'s, wash them in soapy water (mild soap, being careful not to get any water on the label) and then dry with soft tissue. When you're playing them adjust the volume to bass. This and the cleaning abolishes much of the surface noise.

Easy Window-Cleaning

Window-cleaning—car, house, or whatever—can be eased considerably by drying the inside of the windows with a side-to-side movement and the outside of the windows up and down. If there are any streaks, you can easily tell whether they are inside or out.

Some vinegar in the water with which you wash windows or other glassware will leave an after-drying polish.

Best Way to Protect Indoor Slate

Apply boiled linseed oil or paste wax, then polish to a soft shine.

CLOTHING CARE

How to Make Slip-Proof Hangers

Insert large, rubber-headed tacks at the ends of wooden hangers, and dresses and sweaters will stay in place. (Especially useful for children, who tend to hang up clothes carelessly.)

Wrinkle Remover

The U.S. Department of Energy suggests that you try hanging your slightly wrinkled clothes in the bathroom while you take a hot shower. The steam from the shower will often remove your clothes' wrinkles while you wash.

Most Efficient Way to Keep Women's Boots in Order

Install a low brass curtain rod, about 20 inches from the floor, along one side of your clothes closet. Boots can be hung from a rod with clips or pants hangers.

Most Efficient Sewing

When sewing buttons, put a *double* thread through the eye of the needle, pull it through, and knot it. You now have four threads going through the holes, and twice through should do the trick.

When hemming, don't pull the thread all the way through on every stitch. Take three or four stitches, then catch the thread in your hand near the hem and pull it through. You'll be surprised how much time you save.

If you're getting farsighted, buy needles with little notches in the top—one good tug and the thread is through. You can find them in notions departments and dime stores.

Moth-Free Knitting Wool

Keep the moths away from stored wool yarn by pushing a mothball into each skein.

DO-IT-YOURSELF REPAIRS

Most Efficient Projects to do Yourself

The greatest percentage of savings in do-it-your self projects are those where labor would form the major part of the cost of the job if it were done professionally. Painting—particularly such time-consuming paint jobs as windows or elaborate trim—is perhaps the foremost area where the labor materials equation clearly favors the do-it-yourselfer.

Spot-Free Paint Job

Smearing your arms and face with petroleum jelly before undertaking a household painting job makes paint spots on you easier to remove. The same routine applies to painting around hinges or latches on a door, or any other hardware which you want to keep clean. Petroleum jelly rubbed on first rubs off easily later along with any misdirected paint.

Best Way to Keep Your Paintbrush Soft Mid-Job

If you can't finish that paint job, wrap your brush in aluminum foil, whether clean, dry, or full of paint. It will not harden for a week or more. No need for rubber bands to hold the foil in place, either.

How to Unstick Drawers

Spray silicone lubricant on the runners in the chest and on the bottom of the drawers. (It's a good idea to shellac or varnish drawers inside and out to keep them from swelling in humid weather.)

Fastest Way to Oil a Hinge

First, remove the pin. Clean the inside surfaces of the hinge. Apply one or two drops of oil and spread evenly over the entire surface. On hinges from which the pin cannot be removed, apply a drop of oil at the top of the pin and work the hinge back and forth to spread the oil evenly.

Loose Screw

A few drops of peroxide placed on a tight bolt or screw and allowed to soak for a few minutes will help loosen it.

And while the bottlers may not like to admit it, soaking a rusted bolt or screw in Coca-Cola for a while will work loosening magic.

Most Efficient Nailing

Whenever possible, drive a nail on a slant, rather than straight. It will have greater holding power, forming a stronger joint.

To reduce the danger of splitting the wood, stagger nails so no two go through the same length of grain.

Chestnut and maple are less apt to split if you drill a pilot hole first, about half the length of the nail.

Cheapest Sandpaper

You can double the life of your expensive abrasive materials by cleaning them. Use a stiff brush on coated abrasives like sandpaper, garnet paper, or emery cloth. If deposit is hard or gummy, use a metal-bristled file or wire brush.

Fastest Way to Stop Pipes from Rattling

Pad the pipe with rubber wherever it passes through an opening in a wall or floor, and then seal it. This helps cut down on the vibration which causes the noise, and prevents the noise from passing through one room to another.

Shortcut to Keeping Nails Clean While Doing Your Dirty Work

Rub your fingertips over a bar of soap. It will fill the area under your fingernails and keep them clean when you work around grease, paint, or dirt.

No-Stick Bottle Tops

Cold cream or oil used to grease the screw threads of caps on nail polish, glue, and similar items will keep them from sticking.

Keep Rubber Gloves Longer

Second-best way to keep fingernails from punching through rubber gloves is, of course, to cut the nails short. Best way is to stuff some cotton into the ends of each glove finger.

Quickest Way to Fix a Broom Handle

If a screw-on broom handle becomes loose or just won't thread on the broom, try wrapping a little steel wool around the threads and screw tight. You'll find the handle will hold fast.

Best Way to Sharpen a Pair of Dull Scissors

Rub the *outside* of the blades across a flat sharpening stone with even strokes. (Never sharpen inside edges.)

DECORATOR TIPS

Best Way to S-T-R-E-T-C-H Your House

- Put a desk with a comfortable chair and add an easy chair in your bedroom so that you'll use it for a study, informal office, or for entertaining friends in privacy.
- Put a good light over the dining room table for puzzles, games, studying, wrapping gifts, cutting out patterns.
- Put a comfortable chair in the kitchen so you can read or sew while dinner cooks.

Cheapest Way to Unify a Room

Use the same color everywhere—on walls, doors, moldings, slipcovers, even picture mats. Choose a contrasting accent color for pillows, lampshades, and accessories.

Cheapest Way to Make a Small Room Cosy

Paint the walls a dark color, even though the room doesn't get much sun. Dark blue or chocolate brown in a high gloss finish will look stylish and intimate.

Fastest Way to Create Custom-Look Painted Walls

Apply wallpaper borders around ceilings, baseboards, and doorways. Choose colors which blend or contrast with walls, then match border colors with carpets or drapery and upholstery materials.

Easy Ways to Add Elegance with Moldings

Panel plain doors with molding bought at a lumber store. Molding can be antiqued, painted the same color as the door, or highlighted with a different shade. You may want to paper inside the panels to match the walls.

Sometimes two moldings are better than one. Make a dado in a kitchen or dining room, using a large molding on top, smaller beneath.

Do your doorways need more distinction? Add to existing moldings for a richer effect.

Cheapest Way to Dress Up Your Home

New hardware—knobs for cabinet or closet doors, pulls for drawers—gives a fast facelift to kitchen, bathroom, or bedroom. Novel shapes and colors blend with any decorating theme and boost home beauty in a big way for little cost—just a few dollars.

Most Creative Way to Give Your Home an Expensive, Decorator Look

Your own free-hand art on cabinets, doors, or walls will do the trick. Paint a tree at the doorway, paint flowers on your kitchen cabinet doors or a large-scale graphic on the dining area wall. You can even create your own "headboard" if you can't find one you like or can afford.

Easiest Way to Make a Cheerful, Charming Doorway

In a hall or entranceway, paint two red or green

tubs about 18 inches tall on the wall on each side of the door, then cut trailing vines and flowers out of coated paper and paste them on the wall so that they appear to fill the pots and climb to the top of the door.

Cheapest Way to "Cover" a Floor

Paint it. Stencil an all-over pattern or paint it a solid color and create a border to match wallpaper or draperies. Use enamel paints, then varnish and wax, and your custom floor will wear surprisingly well.

DECORATING
ROOM BY ROOM

Cheapest Way to "Tile" a Bathroom

Paint the tile with the new epoxy made to cover ceramic tile. There's a wide range of colors, so be creative: try a Greek key design around the top or paint the shower enclosure a different color from the rest of the room.

Inexpensive Glamor for Your Bed

Make beautiful boudoir pillows from hand-embroidered dresser scarves, hand-crocheted doilies and placemats, old silk scarves. You'll find them in junk shops, rummage and garage sales—or in your aunt's attic.

Cheapest Way to Get a Handsome Bedroom Mirror

Find an ornate old frame in a junk shop, spray paint it with your favorite color, add highlights of gilt and enamel, and have a mirror installed in the lovely new setting.

Best and Fastest Way to Get a Useful Corner Desk

In a bedroom or family room, put a chest of drawers on each wall (one unit might have doors instead of drawers) and cut a piece of plywood to fit over both tops and the space between. Finish with several coats of paint or varnish, or glue a remnant of smooth vinyl flooring in place.

Tips for Linen Closets

- Linen mats, cloths, and napkins should be wrapped in tissue paper or stored in plastic bags to prevent yellowing.
- Separate compartments built into a linen closet, sized for sheets, cases, towels and washcloths, make it easier to keep a closet orderly.
- Sachets, pomanders or bunches of pine or lavender keep linens sweet-smelling. Or unwrap cakes of soap and place among linens.
- Building a new home? A linen closet built into a bathroom is extra-handy. Many existing bathrooms also have room for a closet.
- Need more room for linen? Consider high shelves built over the toilet or over the sink and/or medicine chest for towels and cloths.
- Set aside one shelf in your linen closet for extra stocks of toilet paper, toothpaste, soap, shampoo, and tissues.
- Many linen closets have shelves too far apart to be really handy. If you're stacking sheets and towels too high, ask the handyperson in your family to install an extra shelf or two.
- Make good use of the inside of your linen closet doors. Hang them with shoe bags to store out-of-season shoes and sneakers. Or make bags of your own design out of quilted material and fasten to the back of the door to store napkins and placemats.

Guest Room Tips that Say "Welcome"

- A small bouquet of fresh flowers on the bedside table.
- A jam jar filled with mints.
- A good lamp for reading and two or three current magazines.
- A cosy shawl for reading in bed.

Best Way to Arrange Your Possessions

Group them. A collection of brass or crystal candlesticks, baskets, pitchers, old perfume bottles, antique bottles, shells—anything you collect will make a stronger statement if arranged in one place, such as a tabletop, windowsill, or shelves.

Fastest Way to Cover a Table

Use a quilted bedspread. An elegant, floor-length cover for a bedroom or living room table or even for a dining table can be made from a ready-made quilted bedspread. It will have weight and body, will drape beautifully, and will give you a heatproof top.

Cheapest Way to Make Placemats

Heatproof placemats can be made from quilted material available at any fabric store. Make oval, square, or round mats, finish with binding or trim with rows of nylon ribbon. (Often unquilted matching fabric is available for napkins.)

Fastest Way to Add Bookshelf Space in Your Study

For the home office or the home study area. First, find space in the kitchen or a bedroom. Then pick a wall and apply furring strips. What's a furring strip? It's a strip of wood or other material, and it's intended to support still another material—in this case, prefinished, perforated hardboard. Install per-

forated hardboard panels over the furring strips on
the wall. Insert brackets in the perforations at varying heights. Brackets will hold handsome shelves,
which in turn will hold schoolbooks, cookbooks,
household record books, any books—short, medium
or tall.

Fastest Way to Freshen a Worn Concrete Patio

Use special cement paint available in hardware
and paint stores. Try two colors—tile red and sky
blue, for instance—and paint a design at steps,
doors, or gates.

CHRISTMAS

Best Way to Wrap Christmas Gifts

Assemble everything in one place. Set up a card
table or ironing board that can be left standing if
you have a lot of gifts to wrap.

Use an empty box to keep scissors, ribbons, transparent tape, gift tags, and stickers together and
handy.

Arrange packages according to families and pack
in shopping bags as you go along. Be sure to tag
each gift as soon as it's wrapped to avoid confusion.

Handle each package as little as possible to keep
it looking fresh and pretty.

Best Tips for Christmas Wraps

Pack home-made sweets in reusable containers—
clear plastic shoeboxes, wooden jewelry boxes, small
wicker baskets, handpainted or fabric-covered crack-
er tins or coffee cans.

Save chicken and turkey wishbones throughout
the year, paint with red enamel (nail polish works
well), and add to package bows.

Take odd earings, discarded beads and pins, and
wire them to foil-wrapped gifts.

Cover a box with shiny black paper and glue

bands of red ribbon and gold braid in place for a rich-looking wrap. Especially effective for a man's gift.

Wrap jars of homemade preserves in red-checked shelf paper, pack in a bread basket, cover with clear plastic wrap, and top with a red bow.

Christmas all Through the House

Choose a motif and stick to it—a star, a bird, a heart—and find or make variations of it for walls, tables, and doorways.

Try a two-color tree for impact—pink plastic roses and silver balls; red balls and gold stars; gold balls and red-flocked apples made of styrofoam.

Frame your front door, inside or out, with red and green foil paper chains in a series of graceful swags. Catch them up in the center with a star or a big bow.

Fill a plant rack or stand with Christmas boughs and shining ornaments. Tie a red bow here and there.

In the nursery hang a bright fish kite from the ceiling and suspend six or eight blue, red, and silver balls on nylon thread at different lengths in front of the fish—like bubbles of water.

String Christmas balls on thin wire and surround a mirror, taping the glitter in place at the corners.

Slip a spiky top-of-the-tree ornament over the finial of a lamp, or hook shining silver or gold balls into the inside wire frame of a lampshade.

Let the children decorate the door to their room with Christmas cutouts—a gaily trimmed tree or a fat Santa.

Drape an inside doorway with streamers of brightly colored crepe paper, each one ending with a bell or shiny ornament.

Make a lush wreath for over the mantel. Start with a generous-sized wreath and trim it with wired pine cones, crabapples, tangerines, and small, colorful plastic fruit available in most five-and-dime stores.

Christmas Tree Care and Safety

People who buy real trees for Christmas aren't getting what they pay for if the tree isn't fresh. Check for needles that break when they're bent— dry and brittle needles can mean a fire hazard. A butt that is sticky with resin can indicate freshness; the color of the needles does not.

The tree should last about two weeks, and water loss can be reduced by spraying it with antiwilt material obtainable from a nursery. Cut the tree base an inch or more above the original cut to insure water absorption, and be sure the tree stands in a container that is continually replenished with water.

Once needles start falling on the rug, get the tree out of the house. It's a fire hazard.

Even in the house, keep it away from matches, fireplaces, heating units, candles, and cigarettes.

Make sure tree lights do not touch needles and are nowhere near other flammable objects. Decorations should always be flame resistant.

Chapter 6
INDOOR GARDENING

CUT AND DRIED FLOWERS

Long-lasting Cut Flowers

To make cut flowers last longer, remove any leaves that might be submerged below the water line. Cut off the ends of the stems immediately before placing the flowers in water to expose fresh absorbing tissue.

Best Way to Gather Wildflowers

Carry wet paper towels or a few ice cubes in a plastic bag on your flower-gathering expedition. (Sprinkle the flowers with water if there's a brook nearby.) Then place flowers in the bag and fasten tightly to keep them fresh.

Colorful Flower Arrangement

Mix several drops of food coloring into a glass of water. Place wildflowers like daisies or Queen Anne's lace or any white flowers into the water, and the dye will be absorbed through their stems, producing a beautiful colored flower.

Dried Flowers

Place the blossoms of zinnias, snapdragons, and other flowers in a shoebox and cover them carefully with a mixture of 2 cups white cornmeal and 1 cup Borax. Let stand for three weeks, and the blooms will be preserved with their natural colors intact.

Cheapest Way to Get a Handsome Dried-flower Arrangement

Make it yourself. Look for an unusual container— a tin breadbox, flour can or canister, or an antique hatbox, and fill it with dried celosia, statice, baby's breath, straw-flowers, and bittersweet. Pick and dry what you can, buy the rest at a florist's shop, and fill the box to the brim. Your bouquet will last for years.

HERBS

Windowsill Herb Garden

Spice up your life with a windowsill herb garden. Choose a sunny window and grow herbs (parsley, chives, basil, and thyme are good choices for a start) in small pots. Keep them watered and fertilized regularly, and you can snip off the leaves as you need them.

Cress

Cress, a pepper-grass, is a very fast-growing herb that can be used in salads, soups, or on sandwiches. Soak a sponge in a dish of water and sprinkle the cress seeds liberally on top. Keep the sponge moist by adding water to the dish, and the cress will be ready to eat in a few days.

Easiest Way to Dry and Store Herbs

Pick fresh herbs with stems, put them head down in canning jars with lids off, and dry them in a slow oven. When herbs are thoroughly dried out, just screw tops on and herbs will retain their flavor and aroma.

VEGETABLES

Cheapest Winter Vegetables

The onset of winter doesn't have to mean the end of tasty, fresh vegetables. Many vegetables, such as leaf lettuce and cherry tomatoes, are well suited to being grown indoors in pots and can provide fresh greens all year. Most of the money spent on expensive winter vegetables goes for transportation, packaging, and paying off the middleman; growing your own will eliminate the expense while providing much tastier food.

Basement Salad Garden

The basement is the ideal environment for a year-round salad garden. Place a large shallow tray of good soil under a fluorescent light fixture and grow many types of leafy vegetables, such as lettuce, romaine, chicory, or spinach. These plants do not require a lot of light or heat. However, do be sure to turn the light on, and do so on a regular schedule.

Grow Your Own Bean Sprouts

Bean sprouts are an economical and nutritious food. Place a half-inch layer of mung bean seed (or alfalfa or oats) into a one-quart jar and cover top with cheesecloth held on by a rubber band. Fill the jar half-full of water. One day later invert the jar, draining off the excess water. Stand the jar upside down on a rack, to provide air circulation. They will sprout within four days.

Fastest Parsley

For the fastest sprouting parsley in the West (or anywhere else), soak the hard-shelled parsley seeds in lukewarm water for 24 hours, then dry and plant at once.

Build Your Own Food Dryer

Fresh garden fruits and vegetables make a delicious and nutritious snack when dried or dehydrated.

Start with a wooden box 18 inches square and 24 inches high. Install four 60-watt light-bulb sockets on the floor of the box. Hinge one side to serve as a door, and install removable wire-mesh-bottomed shelves 2 inches apart inside the box, starting 2 inches above the light bulbs. Drill a few small holes in the top and sides to allow some air to circulate. To dry the fruits and vegetables, slice them up and set on the trays. Turn the lights on for several hours.

HOUSE PLANTS

Turning Down the Thermostat?

The following varieties of flowering house plants will thrive in temperatures of 40°-60°: cyclamen, cineraria, calceolaria, and primula.

Most Durable House Plant

The cast-iron plant (aspidistra) is, as its name indicates, one of the most durable house plants. It can tolerate months of neglect, low light, insufficient moisture, and low humidity, and is therefore ideally suited to the modern American home environment. A close runner-up in durability is the "air-fern" which can't be killed because it is already dead!

Sunny Buds

Many flowering house plants (ivy geranium, for example) fail to bloom or bloom poorly if given too little light. Move these plants to a partially shaded area outdoors in the spring and summer for more exposure to light. As soon as buds form, bring the plants back inside where the buds will open and flower normally. (Once you've brought them in, be sure to wash them off to remove outside pests.)

Plant Lights

Insufficient light is a major problem for most flowering house plants, especially during the low-light winter months. A double fluorescent fixture containing ordinary cool-white bulbs placed 8 inches above the tops of the plants will increase their ability to bloom. The lights should be turned off at night, but no rigid schedule need be followed.

Cheapest Treatment for a Lopsided Plant

Return it to the straight and narrow by turning its pot so that the bend is away from the light. Once it becomes upright, remember to rotate it gradually but regularly.

Humid House Plants

The air inside many homes is way too dry for some house plants to grow properly (low humidity is a common cause of leaf drop, especially on rubber plants and gardenias). To increase humidity fill a flat pan with pebbles or marble chips. Add water until the chips are not quite covered. Set the potted plants on this pan, and the evaporating water will bathe the plants in moisture. Add water when necessary.

Forcing Bulbs

To enjoy tulips, daffodils, crocuses, and hyacinths all winter, plant the bulbs in pots in October, and set them outdoors under straw where they won't freeze. Beginning in January, bring a few pots indoors each week, keep them watered, and they will bloom within four weeks, providing a touch of spring during the bleak midwinter months.

Force Poinsettia into Bloom

Many people discard their beautiful poinsettia plants after the holiday season because, even though the plants thrive all year, they will not bloom the following December. This is because the poinsettia comes into flower in response to the short days and long nights characteristic of the autumn months. After the color disappears in early spring, cut back the plant to about 6". Let it grow over the summer. Then in October and November, stimulate flowering of a poinsettia by placing a plastic garbage bag over the plant at 5 P.M. and remove it around 8 A.M. Give it plenty of sunlight and water for the rest of the day and the leaves will soon begin to turn red.

Growing Your Own Pineapple

Choose a healthy-looking pineapple in the market. Slice off the very top with leaves attached, let it dry several days, and set it in a pot of moist sand. Keep the sand moist until roots form, and then give the plant plenty of light. To induce flowering and fruit formation, place the plant (pot and all) in a clear plastic bag along with several apples. A few days later remove the bag: a small pineapple will soon grow from the center of the plant.

Air-layering

A house plant that has become leggy and devoid of lower leaves (a rubber tree, for example) can be air-layered to produce a new, shorter plant. Nick the stem of the plant several inches below the leaf cluster, and insert a toothpick in the cut to hold it open. Wrap moist sphagnum moss around the injured stem, and cover the whole area with clear plastic, taping it to the stem to seal in the moisture. Care for the plant in the usual way until you see roots penetrating through the moss. Then cut the plant off just below the new roots, remove the plastic, and pot it up.

Leaf Cuttings

African violets can be propagated at home from leaf cuttings. Simply cut off a medium-sized leaf and stick it stem end down into a pot filled with sandy soil. Set the pot in a warm shady spot and keep the soil moist (you may want to slip the pot into a plastic bag). A new plant will grow from the base of the leaf.

Leaf-vein Cuttings

Rex and iron cross begonias can be propagated in the following manner: remove a medium-sized leaf and, using a razor, split several veins midway between the base and the leaf edge. Lay the leaf face up on a pot filled with moist sandy soil and hold it down by pinning firmly in place. Set the pot in a warm location out of direct sunlight and keep the sand moist until new plants grow from the leaf surface.

Leaf Sections

Peperomia and other plants can be propagated by leaf sectioning. Cut a leaf in half from side to side. Set the top half (the half that doesn't have a stem) into a pot of sand with the cut side down. Keep it moist and in a warm spot (but out of the sun) until a new plant grows from the base of the leaf.

Stem Cuttings

Many house plants can be easily propagated by taking cuttings. Remove three inches of the growing tip of a Swedish ivy, philodendron, wandering jew, creeping charley, or bridal veil, making sure that there are several leaves attached, and place the bottom third of the stem in a glass of water. Place it in a warm spot out of direct sunlight, and pot it into moist soil as soon as roots appear.

To Sterilize Soil

To sterilize your own garden soil, spread soil in a thin layer on a cookie sheet and bake in 180° oven for 30 minutes. For larger quantities, place soil in a casserole dish and turn oven to 220°. Plunge a meat thermometer into the soil and bake only until temperature reads 180°—any hotter and beneficial soil organisms might be killed.

Leave Room for Water

Never fill a flower pot with soil to the top. Leave an inch or two of space so that when you water, enough water can be added at one time to thoroughly drench the soil.

Vinegar Promotes Rooting

Most cuttings will root more easily if the rooting medium (sand, perlite, or potting soil) is drenched with a solution of 1 teaspoon vinegar in 1 gallon of water immediately before sticking in the cuttings.

Most Efficient Way to Deal with a Dying Plant

If there is any life left, put it inside a plastic bag (after you have eliminated pests or disease as the problem, of course). As the plant begins to perk up, provide it with a growing number of air holes until the day it is ready to make it on its own.

House Plant Rejuvenation

Summertime is the right time to revive droopy or scraggly house plants. Trim back leggy branches and repot into slightly larger container with drainage holes. Bury the pots outdoors in the shade of a maple tree so that the ground level is even with the soil in the pot. Water and fertilize the plants while they are being exposed to the air, wind, and partial sun. Before the first frost in September, lift the pot out of the soil and bring it back indoors. (Wash plant once it's inside to remove pests.)

PLANT BUGS AND PESTS

Washing Off Mites

Spider mites are a constant pest on house plants. These tiny creatures leave telltale webs as they suck the juice from the undersides of leaves. The most efficient way to combat an infestation of mites is to wash them off. Turn the infected plant on its side in the sink and spray water on the leaves until the pests have been washed down the drain. Repeat the treatment one week later to catch any good swimmers.

Another method is to blend a medium-sized onion with one cup of water in a blender, strain, and use as a spray to kill aphids and spider mites.

African Violets

To prevent white spots and streaks on the leaves of African violets, water only with room-temperature water; 100° water is even better.

Aphid Dip

Small house plants infested with aphids should

be immersed for several seconds in a pot of water heated to 125°F.

Quick Cure for Mealy Bugs

Mealy bugs are powdery-white pests that attack African violets, jade, and other indoor plants. To zap them quickly, dip a Q-tip into a bottle of rubbing alcohol and touch the moist tip to the bugs.

Build Your Own Greenhouse

A greenhouse provides the ideal environment for most plants, especially in the early stages of their growth. Plenty of sun, warmth, and high humidity will encourage tiny seedlings to grow and bloom in their natural surroundings. The most efficient greenhouse for the gardener is one which is attached in a lean-to fashion to the south side of an existing structure such as a garage. Nail a two-by-four 8 feet up along the south-facing exterior wall of a garage or shed. Attach several 12-foot two-by-fours on edge at 4-foot intervals along the length of this header, so that they slope to the ground forming a lean-to. Cover the entire structure with .006 mil clear polyethylene sheeting held in place with lath strips. A door in the garage wall provides easy access to the greenhouse. In northern climates a small bottled gas heater with a thermostat set at 40° will keep the greenhouse temperature above freezing during the winter months.

Chapter 7
OUTDOOR GARDENING

GARDEN PLANNING

No Sun?

Vegetable gardens should be located in the full sun. For those of you who have no sunny spot on your property, the U.S. Department of Agriculture (House and Garden Bulletin #163) recommends the following vegetables for a partially shady location: beets, cabbage, carrots, chives, kale, leeks, lettuce, mustard, green onions, parsley, radish, Swiss chard, and turnips.

Intensive Gardening

A small intensively cultivated garden will provide a maximum yield with a minimum of space and work. Plan carefully for a succession of crops from early spring until the first killing frost. Use early-maturing hybrid varieties and have seedlings on hand to plant as soon as older vegetables have been harvested. For example, sow lettuce seed in a small corner of the garden so that seedlings will be ready to transplant as the older heads are used up. Plan for a fall crop of lettuce, spinach, or kale that can go in after peppers or beans are through producing.

Extend Growing Season

Garden soil is often too wet to plant in the early spring, when peas, spinach, and lettuce are ready to be started. If the soil is prepared in the fall, these crops can be off to a good start at the first sign of warm weather. During the month of October, spade or till the garden soil to a depth of 12 inches, working in some peat moss or organic manure. Mound the soil very slightly so that water will run toward the edges, then cover the entire surface with a sheet of plastic, holding it down with rocks. Snow and rain will run off. When the plastic is removed in early spring, the garden will be ready to receive plants.

Plant Near South Wall

In cooler climates, warm weather crops (corn, beans, peppers) will grow faster near the south wall of a house or garage. If this wall is painted white, heat will be reflected into the garden, producing earlier yields.

Container Gardening

Almost any plant can be grown in a container (pot, tub, barrel) if it is given enough water and fertilizer. The smaller the container, the more frequently you will need to water and fertilize it. Container gardening can really save space, and you won't have to worry about too many weeds. Ideal vegetables for container gardens include lettuce, herbs, tomatoes (staked), and several varieties of vegetables especially bred for container cultivation (patio and tiny tim tomatoes, pot luck cucumber, and slim jim eggplant, to name a few).

Protect Garden Tools

Always clean garden tools before storing them for the winter. To protect them against rust, spray the tools with furniture wax, or dip them in drain oil. Never leave fertilizer in a spreader—it will corrode the metal parts.

SOIL

Watering

Infrequent thorough drenching is always preferable to frequent light watering of garden soil. This is because a light spray of water will penetrate only the very top of the soil, encouraging plant roots to grow near the surface where they are more susceptible to drought and cultivation injury. When watering, make sure that at least the top 6 inches of soil is thoroughly soaked.

Leafy Vegetables Need Nitrogen

Vegetables with edible leaves, such as lettuce, cabbage, collards, and spinach, need a high-nitrogen fertilizer to achieve a maximum growth rate. These crops will mature quickly if given a generous feeding of a lawn fertilizer such as 10-6-4, Scott's Turf Builder, or cow manure several times during the growing season.

Weeds Tell a Story

Before breaking ground for a new garden, observe the weed growth to see if the area will need extensive soil preparation. A lush growth of burdocks, goose foot, or pigweed indicates that the soil is rich in nutrients. Thistles and common mullein often grow in poor soil. Cattails and purple loose-strife thrive in wet spots.

Cover Crops

Garden soil that is poor in nutrients or structure can be improved by a technique known as "green manuring," the planting of a cover crop. Sow sweet clover seed in the spring at the rate of 10 pounds per acre and spade it under the following spring. The nitrogen content of the soil will greatly increase. Sweet clover will thrive in poor soil that is not too acid. In acidic soils, sow rye in September at the rate of 2 bushels per acre and turn it under the following spring. Rye does not add much nitrogen to the soil, but it improves soil structure and organic content.

Composting

Composting is a time-honored method for recycling garden waste (leaves, grass, clippings, etc.) so that it can be used to fertilize the garden. Begin a compost pile in an out-of-the-way spot near the garden and add a handful of lime to the center of the pile lower than the edges so that rain water will be captured. Turn the pile with a pitchfork every few weeks to keep it aerated. Use it on the garden only after the compost has turned a dark brown color and resembles peat humus.

Potassium Fertilizer

Wood ashes contain 5 to 10 percent natural potash. Sprinkle ashes on the soil just before the final tilling, never more than ¼ inch deep. Plants may be sidedressed with ashes to add potassium during flower and fruit formation.

Recycle Christmas Tree

Cut the branches from a Christmas tree after the holidays and lay them on top of low-growing perenial plants for winter protection. Since these plants should be mulched only *after* the ground is frozen (because alternate thawing and freezing can cause damage), the timing is just about right for a Christmas-tree mulch.

Newspaper Mulch

Several sheets of newspaper placed between the rows of garden vegetables will hold in the soil's moisture and keep down the weeds. At the end of the growing season, the newspaper can be spaded into the ground to improve the soil structure.

Plastic Mulch

Black polyethylene sheeting makes a quick and easy garden mulch. It is available in long rolls in widths of one, two, and three feet. Simply roll it out over prepared garden soil, and cover the edges with a little dirt to hold them down. Make a hole in the plastic to insert the seeds or transplants, and the mulch will hold down weeds and conserve moisture. If you've had problems with mice in the garden, plastic mulch can be preferable to straw or leaf mulches.

SEEDS AND TRANSPLANTING

Hybrid Plants

The use of hybrid varieties of vegetables and flower plants can greatly increase yields and improve overall crop quality. A hybrid is a plant that has resulted from the cross-breeding of two separate parent strains, hopefully combining the desirable qualities of each. Hybrids have been bred for early

fruiting (Springset tomato), resistance to disease
(Floramerica tomato), size of flower (White cascade
petunia), and flavor (Silver Queen sweet corn).
Proper selection of hybrid seed can result in great
savings of time and effort for the gardener.

Most Efficient Seed Storage

Store your seeds in powdered milk. According to
the magazine, *Organic Gardening,* even such short-
lived seeds as parsley and onion will remain viable
if they are properly stored in powdered milk. First,
stack four opened facial tissues. Next, measure 2
heaping tablespoons of dry milk—from a freshly
opened box—onto a corner of the tissues. Add the
seeds to the milk and fold the tissues, securing the
ends with tape, twist-on ties, or a rubber band.
Keep the package in a tightly sealed jar in the
refrigerator. The milk should be replaced twice a
year and, of course, the seeds should be used as
soon as possible.

Don't Throw Away Old Seed

A packet of last year's seed can easily be tested to
see if it's still good. Place a pinch of the seed between two sheets of paper toweling and put in a
warm location. Keep the toweling moist, and check
after three weeks to see if the seed has sprouted. If
fewer than half have germinated, buy new seed.

Fast Indoor Seed-starter

If cooler house temperatures are making it difficult for you to get your seeds started—try a heating pad. Cover the pad with a fabric-backed vinyl
table mat to prevent the wires from getting wet.
Enclose your seed containers in a plastic bag and
leave them on the pad at a constant temperature of
65° to 70°F, until the first signs of sprouting. Then
gradually acclimate them to the real world and
your chances of having healthy seedlings to transplant are excellent.

Jiffy-7 Pellets

Seeds and young plants can be started quickly in expandable peat pellets, commonly sold under the brand name Jiffy-7. The pellets look like brown checkers, and when submerged in water for a few minutes, they swell up to become a marshmallow-sized container filled with moist nutrient-laden peat moss. Seeds and transplants thrive in them if they're kept watered, and when the plants are big enough, the entire pellet can be planted into the garden with a minimum of transplant shock.

Sowing Small Seeds

When sowing small seeds in the garden, roll out a strip of tissue paper in the bottom of the furrow. This will make the seed visible as you sow it. Fill in the furrow—the tissue will rapidly decompose.

Thinning

Pulling seedlings out by the roots can damage the surrounding plants. Instead, cut unwanted seedlings close to the ground with a pair of scissors.

Plant Late in the Day

Transplants that are set out into the garden late in the day or on a cloudy day will have a chance to recover from transplant shock before they are scorched by the sun. Also, be sure to water the plant thoroughly as soon as it has been transplanted.

To Start Seeds Easily in the Garden

Dig a trench in the garden 1 inch wide and 2 inches deep. Fill it almost to the top with a prepared planting medium such as Jiffy-mix. Sow the seeds and cover with ½ inch vermiculite. Water thoroughly. The seeds will sprout evenly and easily.

Hot Caps

The growing season of many vegetable plants, especially tomatoes, eggplant, and peppers, can be extended by the use of hot caps. They are little plastic tents that are set over each newly planted seedling to provide a mini-greenhouse environment in the early spring, allowing plants to be set out several weeks earlier than usual.

Instant Hot Caps

Cut the bottom off a plastic bleach bottle or cider jug. Set the jug over a newly transplanted seedling to protect it during its first few days of life.

Cold Frames

The cold frame is an essential tool for the gardener who wishes to stretch the growing season and produce earlier yields. A cold frame is simply a large, low box with a glass or plastic lid (this can be an old storm window) that is removed on warm sunny days to allow the plants inside to be exposed to the elements in the early spring. On cold windy days the glass is left on, and on freezing nights the cold frame is covered with a blanket. When the last danger of frost is past, the plants are removed from the cold frame and planted into the garden, as they are already well adjusted to the outside environment.

Hot Beds

If you have access to a cow or horse, try this messy but effective shortcut: build a cold frame 24 inches high. Spread fresh manure onto the bottom 6 inches of the cold frame bed. Cover this with 6 inches of garden soil and set plants on top of the soil. Cover the hot bed with a glass or plastic sash, and the manure will keep the inside temperature warm to promote maximum growth in the early spring.

ABOUT GROWING VEGETABLES

Low-cost Publications

The U.S. Department of Agriculture has published many informative pamphlets and bulletins on the subject of gardening and lawn care. To obtain a list of the available publications, send 50¢ to Superintendent of Documents, Government Printing Office, Washington, D.C., 20402 and ask for *List of Available Publications of the U.S.D.A. Bulletin No. 11.*

Bee Hives

Many flowers and vegetables—especially cucumbers, squash, and melons—are pollinated exclusively by bees. Establish a bee hive near the garden and your yields will improve.

Store Root Crops in the Ground

Beets, carrots, turnips, and parsnips can be stored over the winter without removing them from the garden. Simply cover the plants in November with a heavy layer of mulch—leaves, straw or pine boughs—to keep the ground from freezing. Pull the crops from under the mulch as they are needed during the winter months.

GROWING FRUIT
AND VEGETABLES A TO Z

Beet Tops

Sow beet seed liberally in the garden, raking it into the top half-inch of soil. Allow the beets to grow 6 inches high before thinning: then use the plants that are thinned out as beet tops for cooking or in salads. Let the remaining beets grow to maturity.

Planting Carrots

Heavy, rocky soil can be terrible for carrots, causing splitting and forking of the roots. In heavy soils use short stubby varieties (Baby fingers or Danvers). Or else dig a V-shaped trench 12 inches deep and fill the trench with a mixture of half sand and half peat moss. Add a little bone meal or other fertilizer. Then sow the carrot seeds on top and the roots will thrive in the loose sandy soil.

Blanching Celery and Endive

Celery growing in the garden needs to be "blanched" to keep the white stalks from becoming green and tough. An easy method for blanching celery: when the plants are 8 inches tall, place a one-by-six-inch wooden board on either side of the row; drive pegs into the ground to hold the boards tight up against the plants. This will allow the stalks to turn white by keeping the sunlight out. Endive can be blanched simply by laying a board right on top of the row of plants.

Collards

This member of the cabbage family is much easier to grow than its close relatives broccoli, cauliflower, cabbage, and kale, and it contains all their nutritional value. Collards will not turn to seed in hot summer weather and can withstand frosts down to 10°F.

Corn

Never plant corn in long, single rows. It is wind-pollinated, so the ears will be more fully developed if the stalks are planted in a block of several short rows or in "hills" of four to six stalks placed 3 feet apart.

Take a Tip From the Indians

The American Indians saved space in their vegetable garden by sowing lima bean seed at the base of each corn stalk when the corn was about knee high. The bean plants were trained to climb up the corn stalks, and at harvest time—instant succotash!

Clear Plastic Mulch for Corn

Sow corn seed 8 inches apart in double rows 12 inches apart, allowing 3 feet between each double row. Cover the double rows with clear plastic film, burying the edges of the film in the soil to hold them down. Let the seed germinate and grow underneath the plastic until the corn stalks are several inches high. Then slit the plastic, allowing the stalks to unbend and grow to maturity. Early corn grown in this way will often be ready to eat in the Northeast by June 30.

Pea Brush

Plant peas very early in the spring so that they can get a jump on the weeds. Instead of providing an expensive trellis or plastic netting for the pea vines to climb on, gather some sturdy twigs, each about 2 feet long, and stick them into the soil several inches apart, next to the rows of peas. The vines will cling to the twigs and provide support for the ripening pods.

Solution to the "No Pepper Problem"

Pepper plants are notorious for their habit of producing an abundance of lush green foliage but no fruit. To prevent this problem, plant only in full sun, apply fertilizer sparingly after plants are established, and grow only varieties that are recommended for your area (Ace and Staddon's Select are excellent in the Northeast).

Freeze Peppers

Peppers are the simplest garden vegetable to freeze. One need only rinse the fresh peppers, cut them into pieces, place them in a plastic bag, and pop them into the freezer. Once thawed they are delicious for use in sausage and pepper sandwiches or pepper and onion dishes.

Early Spinach

Sow spinach in the late fall, raking the seed into the top half-inch of well-worked, fertilized garden soil. The seed will germinate with the first spring thaw, allowing a spinach harvest before any weeds or pests have time to compete with the crop.

Hot-weather Spinach

Spinach turns to seed in hot weather. In summer months spinach fanciers should grow only New Zealand spinach (Tetragonia expansa), which is similar to spinach but will tolerate any amount of heat without turning to seed.

Squash—Easiest Vegetable to Store

Winter squashes are the easiest vegetables to store. Simply harvest when they are ripe in the fall, being careful not to bruise them or cut the skins, and set them in a place where the temperature remains around 55°F (40°–70°F will do)—underneath the kitchen sink, for example. They will remain fresh and ready to eat for many months. The winter squash family includes butternut, acorn, buttercup, and blue hubbard.

Weeding Strawberries

A small flock of geese let loose in the strawberry patch in early May, before the fruit begin to develop, will do a good job of weeding. Geese enjoy snacking on weeds, but have no preference for strawberry plants.

Tomato—Most Economical Garden Vegetable

This long-standing favorite will produce fruit under a wide variety of soil conditions and climates. One hybrid plant can yield up to a hundred tomatoes if properly cared for, and, when staked, can be grown in a space just 4 feet square.

Tomato Cages

A tomato "cage" can be built from a section of four-by-four-inch welded wire fencing, 4 feet wide and 8 feet long. Form the fencing into a cylinder 4 feet high and place it around the tomato plant after it has been set into the garden. The cage will provide support for the growing plant, and the ripening fruit will be kept up off the ground. Tomatoes are harvested by reaching through the openings in the fencing.

Most Efficient Tomato Plant

If you are setting a tomato transplant into the garden, choosing the proper size plant will save time and increase yield. A plant that is less than 6 inches tall will take added time to mature; a large plant that is already sporting flowers or small fruit will mature quickly but yield poorly. The ideal plant is 6 to 12 inches tall with a thick but soft stem and no blossoms, growing in a 3- or 4-inch peat pot.

To Plant Tall Tomato Plants

Tomato transplants with long stems will thrive in the garden if handled properly. Dig a short trench 4 to 6 inches deep and lay the plant on its side, curving the stem upward so that the top leaves stick out of the ground. Fill in the trench, burying the long stem. New roots will grow from the covered stem and the plant will be stronger. This method should also be used when planting cabbage, broccoli, and cauliflower seedlings.

Ripening Green Tomatoes

Harvest green tomatoes just before the first autumn frost. Store them in a basket in a cool dark location. An apple placed amid the tomatoes will release a small amount of ethylene gas that aids and speeds up the ripening process.

Quick Watermelons

The watermelon is usually considered a long-season crop. However, the "sugar baby" variety, which matures quickly to yield sweet juicy melons the size of a bowling ball, is suited for northern climates. The fruits are often called ice-box watermelons because they are small enough to be stored in the refrigerator.

ANIMALS AND PESTS

Scarecrow

String aluminum pie pans on a rope and hang it between two poles in the garden. Birds will be scared away.

Bird-proof Fruit

Strawberries, cherries, and other fruit will be inaccessible to birds if a very fine, wide-mesh netting is draped over the plants or trees while fruit is ripening.

To Control Cabbage Worms

Dissolve a tablespoon of salt in 2 gallons of water. Spray on cabbage, broccoli, or cauliflower plants to control green cabbage worms.

Cabbage Butterfly

There is some evidence that mint planted in the vicinity of cabbage plants will repel the cabbage butterfly. Plant the mint in carefully controlled small pots to keep *it* from taking over the garden.

Kill Corn Earworms

A drop of mineral oil placed on the silk of a newly emerged ear of corn will protect it against corn earworms. For maximum protection, repeat the treatment every four days until the silk turns brown.

Cutworm Bait

Mix molasses, wheat bran, and hardwood sawdust into a thick paste and pour it in a ring around plants that are susceptible to cutworm attack. The worms will be attracted to the bait and it will stick to their bodies, rendering them helpless.

Cutworm Collar

The garden cutworm crawls just beneath the surface of the soil, chomping its way through the stems of pepper plants and other garden crops. To stop the cutworm cold in its tracks, use a cutworm collar. Cut the top and bottom off a tin can, then cut the can into "collars" 3 inches wide. At planting time, push the collars into the ground around each plant to be protected, allowing 1 inch to show above the soil surface.

Dust for Flea Beetles

Flea beetles will not chew the leaves of tomato or eggplant if they are dusted lightly with ground limestone.

Gopher-proof Garden

To keep moles and gophers out of a raised garden, lay ½-inch wire mesh screening over the entire bottom of the garden before adding the planting soil.

Japanese Beetle Traps

A new Japanese beetle trap is available that promises to control these pests. It uses as its bait a tiny amount of a pheremone, which is the mating chemical of the female beetle. This powerful attractant steers thousands of male beetles into the trap. A floral scent in the trap attracts female beetles. The device is being marketed under the brand name "Bag-a-bug."

To Scare Rabbits

Rabbits are sometimes scared away from the garden by a row of glass bottles stuck neck down into the soil at the garden's edge. Even more effective is a row of small plastic pinwheels on sticks.

Rabbit Repellant

Dried blood sprinkled near plants will repel rabbits.

Snail Bait

Snails and slugs love to chomp on the leaves of flowers and vegetables, but there is nothing they like better than marigolds. So a border of marigolds around the outside edge of the garden will waylay the slimy pests on their nightly foray. They will stop to feed on the marigolds and not bother to venture any further.

Easy Protection from Root Maggot

The root maggot is a serious pest on broccoli, cabbage, and cauliflower. These tiny white worms chew the roots, causing the plant to wither even if the soil is moist. A drench with diazinon spray a week after planting (follow label directions) will help cure the problem, but a quick way to prevent an infestation is to cut a cardboard circle 12 inches across with a slit from center to edge and place it around the plant so that it rests on the ground and the plant stem sticks up through the center. This will prevent the adult maggot fly from laying its eggs in the ground at the base of the plant.

Birds Fight Pests

Attract insect-eating birds to the garden by placing in the garden a bird feeder containing suet cakes.

Mantis Egg Cases

The praying mantis eats many harmful garden pests. Egg cases are produced in the fall—small oval-shaped (Carolina mantis) or rounded masses of brown foam that stick to a board or plant stem. If you find a mantis egg case while you're cleaning up the yard, tie it with a piece of thread to a stick and poke it into the garden soil. Come spring, the tiny mantis will crawl out and protect your crops.

FLOWERS

Perennial Flowers

Perennial flowers bloom year after year, and if they are planted properly will afford years of trouble-free splendor. In planning a perennial garden, choose varieties that bloom at different seasons of the year, so that color will abound from spring through fall. The peony is one of the most long-lived and beautiful perennials. Peony plants have been known to blossom for hundreds of years even on abandoned property.

Refrigerate Snapdragon Seeds

Germination of snapdragon seeds will be greatly

improved if they are placed in the refrigerator for 48 hours before sowing.

Naturalizing Bulbs

Crocus, narcissus, and other long-lasting garden bulbs are often "naturalized"—that is, planted in a lawn or garden setting to look as if they grew there naturally. Place the bulbs in a basket, then gently toss them out of the basket toward the area where the bulbs are to be planted, as if you were tossing water from a wash bucket. Plant each bulb where it falls. If you are naturalizing a lawn area, do not mow the grass until late June, to give the bulbs a chance to grow before their foliage is cut off.

Dividing Perennials

Many perennial plants (iris, english daisy, day lilies and others) can be propagated simply by digging up clumps of roots in the late fall, cutting them into fist-sized pieces and moving them to new locations in the garden. In fact, if they are not divided every few years, they can become so crowded that flower production will be reduced.

Disbudding

Show-size cut flowers are produced by a process known as disbudding. Flowering plants, especially chrysanthemums and peonies, often have more than one flower on a stalk. If you want only one large bloom per stalk, remove all the buds except the largest (usually the topmost) one.

Pinch Them Back

Tall, leggy annual flowers can be pinched back to produce stocky, bushy plants. Simply remove the very tip of the plant, making sure to leave at least three leaf nodes on the remaining stem. This can be done at transplanting time to leggy seedlings, or later on to give tired lanky flowers a new lease on life.

Pest-free Flower

The begonia, a beautiful flower that will tolerate partial sun or shade, is rarely bothered by garden pests.

TREES AND SHRUBS

To Water Newly Planted Trees

After planting a tree or shrub, scrape soil from the surrounding area to form a low circular ridge a foot or two from the center of the plant. This ridge will make it much easier to thoroughly water the newly planted shrub, because it will form a dish into which the water can be poured.

Pollination

Certain varieties of fruit trees (Queen Anne cherry, for example) will not bear fruit unless pollinated by another variety of tree. If such a tree is available but not nearby, get several flowering branches from it and place them in a pail of water near the tree to be pollinated. Bees will visit the bouquet and carry the pollen to your tree.

Dwarf Fruit Trees

An ordinary pear tree may need five years to come into bloom, but a dwarf tree will bear within two years. Dwarf fruit trees are a boon to the gardener—they provide fruit equal in size and quality to that of full-size trees but require a minimum of space. Be sure to keep the bud union (where the tree has been grafted to its dwarf root-stock) above the soil line when planting.

Keep Shrubs Full-looking

Most shrubs, especially evergreens, should be trimmed to keep the base slightly wider than the top. This prevents the top branches from shading the lower ones so that their leaves fall off causing bare spots.

Forsythia Branches

Prune forsythia bushes in early March, just as the new buds are beginning to swell. Place the cut branches in a vase indoors and the buds will soon open, creating a lovely display of yellow blooms.

Layering

Many types of shrubs and woody plants can be layered to produce new plants. Choose a young branch of yew, juniper, forsythia, or other plant and nick a piece of bark from the underside, or tear the bark by removing a leaf. Dig a shallow trench in the ground and bend the branch down so that the injured area touches the bottom of the trench. Hold it down by shoving a forked stick firmly over it into the ground, and cover the branch with soil. Several months later roots will form from the wounded area. When the branch is firmly rooted, it can be severed from the parent bush, dug up and replanted elsewhere.

Fastest Way to Plant a Willow Tree

Cut a 6-foot branch from an established willow tree and stick it into the ground in a moist shady area. It will soon send out roots and mature into a healthy tree.

Preventing Winter Injury

One of the most frequent causes of winter injury among plants and shrubs—especially among rhododendrons, azaleas, and other broadleaf evergreens—is desiccation. Strong winter winds can cause transpiration of the plant's moisture through its leaves when the ground is either too frozen or too dry to provide replacement moisture to the roots. To prevent desiccation injury, thoroughly soak the ground around the shrubs in late autumn just before it freezes, and apply mulch at the base of the plants.

Another quick way to accomplish this is to surround the shrub with a cylinder made from chicken wire. When raking the lawn, fill the cylinder with leaves. They will keep the shrub warm until early spring, when the cylinder is removed and the leaves fall down to provide a protective mulch at the base of the plant.

Protect Tree Trunks

Deer, rabbits, and mice love to chew the bark of tender fruit or ornamental trees during the lean winter months (the damage may not be apparent until the snow thaws). Protect the trees with a girdle of 1-inch wire mesh around each trunk from the ground to a height of 3 feet.

Snow—the Gardener's Friend

Snow is nature's blanket. It covers the ground during the coldest winter months, protecting small bushes from the wind and preventing the deep penetration of frost into the ground. Use snow to your advantage by shoveling it onto perennial plants and around the trunks of shrubs, especially if the wind has created a bare patch in the garden. An early snowfall will keep the frost from penetrating beds of tulip bulbs too deeply, so mound the snow up over these areas.

Landscape to Save Energy

Plant evergreen trees on the north side of a house (50 feet from the house) for protection from cold winter winds. Deciduous trees planted in the south

lawn will provide shade in the hot summer months;
in the winter they'll lose their leaves, letting the
sun through to warm the house.

YOUR LAWN

Cut Down on Watering Time

Place a coffee can or other straight-walled container under your lawn sprinkler before you water
the lawn. Leave the sprinkler running only until
there is one inch of water in the can; any additional
water on the lawn is unnecessary.

Easier Lawn Mowing

Keep driveways, patios, and sidewalks flush with
the lawn surface for easier lawnmowing. Place a
12-inch wide brick strip around trees and shrub
areas to eliminate the need to trim.

Eliminate Crabgrass

Crabgrass is a symptom, not a cause, of a poorly
tended lawn. Since crabgrass is an annual plant, it
can only reseed itself on bare spots where new
seedlings can become established. Proper lawn care,
including fertilization and seeding of bare spots
with a good seed, will choke out crabgrass without
the need for expensive and dangerous chemical
controls.

Most Efficient Way to Kill Dandelions

If you can't take time to dig dandelions out of
your yard, a drop of kerosene on each plant will
kill it immediately. Blossoms should be touched
too.

Chapter 8
EDUCATION AND CAREER

SHORTCUTS TO SUCCESS

Fastest Way to Change Your Life

Give up these words:
Try, always, everybody, can't, should, why.

Efficient Way to Organize Yourself

Your list is your best friend. Take it wherever you go, and tick off each item you accomplish. Look at organization as a game. See how many items you can finish each day, and carry over the unfinished ones into the next day. Start out with the small things first, such as returning someone's phone call in the morning. Then you can build up momentum as you go along.

Efficient Way to Stop Procrastinating

In order to stop procrastinating, you have to realize its futility. You have to want to be more responsible, which means you have to want to begin to "win." To stop being overwhelmed by what you have been avoiding, break down your tasks into a daily schedule. For instance, you can write a 200-page book in seven months, writing one page each day. Realize that unpleasant or difficult tasks are problems that you have to solve. Write down on a piece of paper possible ways to solve each difficult problem. Make deadline commitments, and figure out a personal reward for keeping them. List the good things that can happen by your accomplishing your task.

STUDY HABITS

Most Efficient Way to Take Notes

When making notes for a term paper or other written presentation, take the notes on note cards rather than in a note book. That way, with one thought, quote, or figure on each note card, they can be readily organized into whatever form your project requires. You'll find that simply by arranging the cards in a coherent order, many of your papers will all but write themselves.

Most Efficient Way to Study a Textbook

Check to see if the book (or chapter) you're studying has a review at the end. If so, study it first—*before* you read the material itself. The review will tell you what the most important points to be covered are. Then go back and read the book with these important points in mind. If the book doesn't have a review, study the table of contents first. You'll find that this review-first method will not only help you to fix the main points firmly in your mind, but will help you to understand how the rest of the material relates to and amplifies them.

Most Efficient Order for Homework

When you have several courses to study for, it is best to work on the hardest subject first, while your mind is still fresh.

Most Efficient Way to Memorize

Don't just repeat what you want to memorize to yourself, and don't just write it down. Do both. Whatever it is you want to memorize, whether it's in words or figures, write it out in longhand, and *repeat it as you write.* The two actions will reinforce each other and enable you to memorize faster and retain what you learn more effectively.

Surest Way to Become a Good Writer

Writing is not something that can be learned from reading a book; it is a skill that must be developed through constant practice. One of the best ways to improve your writing is to write for a newspaper, preferably one that is relatively small and willing to give a beginner the opportunity to write a great deal. Your writing should become more precise and your writing speed will improve dramatically.

SCHOOL AND COLLEGE

Easiest Way to Find the Best School for Your Child

As a general rule, says a consultant at an advisory service for private schools in business for forty years, the smaller the school, the more attention your child will receive. Optimally, the maximum student population should be no more than 500, if you're paying tuition at an elementary-through-high-school private school. (A similar criterion can be applied to your local public school.)

Look for small class size, a sprinkling of younger teachers mixed with older more experienced teachers, good physical equipment, regents' accreditation, availability of headmaster or principal and staff to students and parents, and what schools and colleges the graduates attend. Talk to the principal or headmaster. If you like him/her, chances are you'll like the school's philosophy.

But the best school is still the one the *child* likes. If the child is self-confident, feels comfortable, and is learning, you've chosen well.

Cheapest Private Schools

In general, denominational schools, such as Roman Catholic parochial schools, charge lower tuition fees than nonsectarian schools. This is also true on the college level. In some cases, tuitions are lower for members of the sponsoring denomination.

Teenagers' Best Bet for Summer

College. Every summer outstanding universities across the country accept high school students for summer courses, many for low fees, some of them without charge. Established for students who wish to pursue their special field of interest, the courses often are not well publicized and counselors may not know about them. Usually lasting six weeks, they provide excellent preparation for Scholastic Aptitude Tests and Achievement Tests, as well as a preparatory experience in college living. For information, contact the admissions office at the university or universities of your choice.

Easiest Way to Get a High School Diploma

Take a high school equivalency test. The test measures four years of high school learning skills:

1. Writing skills
2. Social studies (economics, current events, political science, and behavioral science)
3. Science (chemistry, biology, earth science, and physical science)
4. Reading skills
5. Mathematics (arithmetic, geometry, algebra)

High schools, church and other adult groups throughout the country have free tutorial programs available. Tests are administered by local boards of education. Pass the test and you receive a GED (Graduate Equivalency Diploma).

Another method, which bypasses the test, is a new program being developed at community colleges. You attend community college, complete twenty-four credits—with good grades—and are granted the GED. (The rationale: successful completion of upper level courses indicates your life experience background fulfills the GED requirement.)

GETTING INTO COLLEGE

Surest Way to Hike Standardized Test Scores

The standardized tests administered by the Educational Testing Service have a tremendous influence over where students go to school on the undergraduate or graduate level. In fact, in certain fields like law and medicine, the tests can often determine whether students get admitted anywhere. The testing service has traditionally discouraged students from taking special courses to prepare for the tests. However, the Federal Trade Commission has found, after a lengthy study, that some of these courses can actually improve the test performance of students whose scores on standardized exams are well below their grades in class. The Stanley Kaplan Testing Agency was singled out as being particularly effective in hiking test scores of students. There are approximately ninety Kaplan centers in the United States and Canada, as well as one in Switzerland.

Easiest Ivy League School to Get Into

An Ivy League diploma is often a ticket to the good life of high wages, social status, and security. It remains rather difficult, however, to get into one of the so-called Ancient Eight (Brown, Columbia, Cornell, Dartmouth, Harvard, Penn, Princeton, or Yale). Undoubtedly the easiest to get into is the University of Pennsylvania. The Philadelphia school accepts roughly 45 percent of those applying to its freshman class. Columbia and Cornell accept about 40 and 36 percent of those applying, respectively, while the other Ivies accept a significantly smaller percentage.

Easiest Way to Get an Ivy League Education

The easiest way to get an Ivy League degree is to go to Brown University in Providence, Rhode Island. In fact, the hardest thing about Brown is just getting in—almost 12,000 high school seniors apply annually for approximately 1,300 places in the freshman class. Almost everyone who matriculates eventually receives a degree. (The attrition rate of 2–3 percent is among the lowest in the nation.)

Undergraduates at Brown are only required to pass twenty-eight courses over a four-year period in order to graduate, and none of these courses have to be taken for grades. Each student has the option of taking any of his courses on a satisfactory/no credit basis. In addition, there are no distribution requirements and no required courses, with the possible exception of an introductory writing course for students who do very poorly on the verbal section of the Scholastic Aptitude Test. Brown may still be more demanding than many colleges across the country, but it is simply not as demanding as the other Ivies, some of which require students to pass thirty-six courses and write senior theses in order to graduate.

Surest Way to Get into Medical School

Medical school has traditionally been one of the most difficult professional schools to get into. Just a few years ago, only about thirty-five percent of those applying to medical school ever got accepted. The percentage has increased slightly over the past few years, but it still remains tough to get in anywhere in the United States. Surprisingly enough, North Dakota and South Dakota universities place a higher percentage of their premeds in medical school than any other schools in the nation. This is primarily because almost all of the premeds at these two schools either already are or eventually become state residents in either North or South Dakota. If they maintain an acceptable average, they are virtually guaranteed a place in their state medical school, since these schools place a premium on state residency in making their admissions decisions.

Fastest Way to Attend Oxford

It may be to enroll in a program of the University of California Extension. They offer a number of study programs for adults in foreign countries. In 1980, for example, it's possible to study screenplay writing in London, the history and natural science of Kenya—on the spot, Minoan and Mycenaean archeology in Greece and Crete, or any one of twenty-eight different courses in historic Oxford University taught by the fabled Oxford dons. Other programs were available from Israel to the Caucasus.

For information, write to the International Department C-70, University of California Extension, 2223 Fulton Street, Berkeley, California 94720.

FINANCIAL HELP FOR COLLEGE

Most Efficient Way to Get Financial Aid at Your College

Most U.S. colleges and universities determine your need through a Financial Aid Form (FAF) administered by the College Scholarship Service (CSS). Contact CSS, Box 2700, Princeton, New Jersey, 08540, or CSS, Box 380, Berkeley, California 94701, for the forms. Once you've received a determination from them they'll send you the FAF. (Keep a Xerox of your FAF with you.) Then consult the financial aid office at your college. They'll help you apply for the type of aid available to meet your financial needs. (Note: most scholarships are awarded for one year and must be renewed by reapplying each year.)

The Undergraduate Rule of Thumb

Never assume you are ineligible for a scholarship or some form of financial aid. There's always money available to assist you to pay college expenses. Check your college catalogue. Thumb through to the pages listing scholarships and grants available through the financial aid office. Then apply, apply, apply.

Easiest Way to Get a Scholarship

Apply for admission to the more exclusive colleges, says a New York college advisory service. The more exclusive the college, the easier it will be for you to get financial assistance—provided your grades are up to snuff and you have good academic credentials. Major universities like Harvard, Yale, Princeton, and Columbia are heavily endowed and well financed. Once they've accepted you, it's their job to help finance your education. They'll not only provide scholarship funding, but their expert financial counselors will help you determine, down to the last penny, what additional expenses you'll need to cover during your four-year college career.

Fastest Federal Scholarship Information

The federal government is involved in many programs designed to provide scholarships, loans, and work-study arrangements for students in post-secondary education. These programs cover many types of educational programs, from vocational training to postgraduate work.

For detailed information on the wide variety of aids available, write to the Office of Education, Department of Health, Education and Welfare, 400 Maryland Avenue SW, Washington, D.C. 20202.

Free Money from BEOG for College Expenses

BEOG (Basic Educational Opportunity Grants), a federally funded financial aid program administered by the U.S. Office of Education, will provide money to help pay for tuition and other college-related expenses. You can even receive pocket money to cover chewing gum (if the gum is a college-related expense)! According to USOE, a Basic Grant is an outright gift of money. "You do not have to pay them back," notes USOE. It's the biggest student aid program and "the starting point for most students seeking federal study money." You don't have to be a scholar to get a BEOG. You must only prove financial need—not difficult in these days of escalating college costs. To apply, you must be a matriculated (undergraduate) student at an accredited college on at least a half-time basis and eligible under the financial formula applied to all applicants. (The Basic Grant Formula is approved annually by Congress.) The *formula*: they assess the information on your application to produce an *eligibility index number*. The number determines the actual amount you'll get.

SER (Student Eligibility Report) is the official notification of your eligibility index number for a Basic Grant (BEOG). The lower the number, the higher the award. When applying for a Basic Grant, if you don't receive the SER within 6 weeks write: Basic Grants, P.O. Box H, Iowa City, Iowa 52230.

Current yearly awards range from $200 to $1800 and they're renewed annually, usually for up to four years of study. (But there are exceptions: if your undergraduate program requires noncredit remedial courses or you're enrolled in a five-year first degree college program.)

Grants are credited to your college account. Whenever your credits exceed the amount you owe the school, according to the program's administrators, you're entitled to a refund from the college (that's your chewing gum money).

Easiest Way to Find Out How Eligibility Index Formula is Computed

While it may not be pertinent, a glance through *Determination of Basic Grant Eligibility Index*, a pamphlet which describes the formula in detail, might assist you in answering the BEOG application form. Write to BEOG, P.O. Box 84, Washington, D.C. 20044 for the pamphlet.

How Federal BEOG Grant Money is Paid to You for Additional Expenses

According to the U.S. Office of Education, a separate check is *not* sent to each student. The money is credited to the college, and the college either credits your award toward your account or gives you a check (or a mixture of both). They must notify you in writing of payment methods of the expected amounts. Most schools are required to pay you the excess over the amount needed for your tuition and fees at least once per term during the academic year.

Easiest Way to Get a BEOG Grant Application

BEOG is administered by the Basic Grants Center in Iowa City, Iowa. Call the Student Information Center, *toll free* at (1) 800-638-6700 any Monday through Friday, 8:30 A.M. to 6:00 P.M. They'll provide general phone information and send application forms by mail. The forms should arrive within a week to ten days. (You can phone them back and they'll explain how to fill out and file the form.)

What's A SEOG?

According to the U.S. Office of Education, SEOG (Supplementary Educational Opportunity Grant) is tax-free money for exceptionally needy undergraduate students. Usually, if you get a SEOG, "it's part of a 'package' that will include additional kinds of financial aid," says the U.S. Office of Education. You apply through your school's financial aid office. The rules are: "No SEOG can be more than half your total aid 'package.' " (An example: a $1,000 SEOG must be matched by at least $1,000 from other aid programs.)

Who's Eligible for a CWS?

CWS (College-Work Study Program) provides jobs and helps you earn part of your college expenses, says the U.S. Office of Education. To apply, you must be at least a half-time (courses equivalent to half a regular program) matriculated student in a college with an eligible CWS program. Undergraduate students receive hourly wages. Graduate students may receive either a salary or hourly wages. A CWS job award is set by the college's aid office (based on financial need) and must always be for a public or private nonprofit agency.

Scholarships While Attending Out-of-State Colleges

State-funded scholarships, offering awards as high

as $2,000, are available in many states. You're eligible even if you're attending an out-of-state college, if you maintain a legal permanent address in your home state (your parents' address is sufficient). Requirements vary, so contact your home state's Department of Higher Education (most are located in the state capital).

Free College Tuition for Veterans and Their Families

A veteran who served at least 180 days in the Armed Forces between January 31, 1955, and January 1, 1977, is entitled to benefits for full-time (and, in most cases, part-time)study at an accredited institution. (The proviso is, you must begin studying less than ten years after release from service and not after December 31, 1989.)

The current program: Veterans Administration Educational Benefits (VETS) provides one and a half months of benefits (up to forty-five months) for each month of active service.

Children, spouses, and survivors of eligible veterans, who either have service-connected permanent disabilities, are listed as missing in action, or whose death was service-connected, are eligible for college benefits under the same conditions as veterans.

The VA office, active duty station, or American Embassy in your area has application forms.

Cheapest Student Loans

NDSL (National Direct Student Loan) provides up to $5,000 for four years of study, at 3 percent (current) interest, payable during a ten-year repayment period. The borrowed money is not repaid until nine months after graduation or leaving school. The minimal monthly payment is $30. You pay interest only on the unpaid balance (principal) of the loan, says the U.S. Office of Education. Apply through your college's financial aid office.

Low Interest Federal Loans for Part-time Undergraduate Students

GSL (Guaranteed Student Loan Program), sponsored by U.S. Office of Education, is available in most states. To qualify you must be: (1) a matriculated student designated a half-time status student (i.e., sufficient courses to equal half a regular program); (2) U.S. citizen or permanent resident alien.

You can borrow up to $2,500 per class year to a maximum of $7,500. A 1 percent annual insurance premium (on loan amount) is deducted from your first check. The current interest rate is 7 percent. You don't repay the loan while you're a half-time student. Four months after either completion of a degree or ceasing studies, you begin repayment. You have up to fifteen years from the initial loan date to repay, and can repay in whole or in part at any time (the latter cuts your interest cost).

Heal Money for Doctors

Want to be a doctor, dentist, veterinarian, pharmacist? Try a HEAL loan. HEAL (Health Education Assistance Loan) is a federally insured loan made to full-time students at HEAL program schools, according to the U.S. Office of Education. If you're seeking the following degrees, you're eligible for HEAL: doctor of medicine, osteopathy, dentistry, optometry, veterinary medicine, podiatry, and/or a graduate (or equivalent) degree in public health, or a bachelor or master of science in pharmacy.

Up to $10,000 per academic year to a total of $50,000 may be borrowed. (Pharmacy students are limited to $7,500 yearly up to $37,500.) Repayment begins nine months after completion of formal training (internship and residency is included) or when you cease full-time student status. You pay interest while in school, but the interest can be accrued and you have ten to fifteen years to repay the loan.

Interest may not exceed 12 percent on unpaid balance. In some instances you can either defer or cancel repayment—if you serve in the National Health Service Corps or have a private practice in a health manpower shortage area, you can apply for federal payments of the loan.

Tax-deductible Tuition Fees

A number of states now permit a tax deduction for tuition paid for college (and, sometimes, private elementary-through-high-school fees). New York state, for example, passed such a law in 1978. Check with your state's income tax bureau. Your parents may be eligible for a tax deduction for your tuition and costs in sending you to college.

Fastest Source of Supplemental Income for College

If even one of your parents is eligible for Social Security, you may qualify for some Social Security benefits yourself—benefits that could help put you through college. Check with your Social Security office.

Easiest Way to Avoid Paying Tuition at Graduate School

It's easier to get a free master's or doctoral degree than a bachelor's. Most universities have fellowships and assistantships for graduate students that are not filled (because no one applies for them). Decide where and what you'd like to study. Write the chairman of the selected university department (listed in the college catalogue). Always address the chairman as professor. Spell his/her name correctly. Say you're impressed by the department's excellent reputation and want to study under his/her tutelage. Follow up with a personal phone call, and then a thank-you letter which says you're being considered by another prestigious university and would appreciate a swift decision since you'd prefer to study with him/her.

Cheapest College

The least expensive college in the United States is also the smallest and one of the most isolated. California's Deep Springs College, located on 2,500 acres of land near the Nevada border, has an enrollment of nineteen—all with full tuition, room and board, and expenses paid. The unusual campus is also a working ranch founded by Lucien B. Nunn, a gold miner, who envisioned a work-study program where exceptional students could earn their keep by running the ranch. It takes more than muscle to qualify, however. Deep Springs students rank among the nation's top 1 percent, and when they complete their two-year stint at the junior college, they commonly move on to the Ivy League.

California has other cheap colleges, though without the academic clout. The College of Alameda costs $4.00 per year; Porterville College in Porterville and Sierra College in Rocklin cost $7.00; and San Joaquin Delta College costs $10.00.

Outside California the cost is steeper, but with residency you can attend St. Bernard Parish Community College in Chalmette, Louisiana, for $55.00 per year, or Bossier Parish Community College in Bossier City, Louisiana, for $60.00.

Cheapest Way to Go to Law School

If you want to go to a law school approved by the American Bar Association but have very limited funds for your legal education, your best bet is to settle in Arkansas, Oklahoma, or West Virginia. The two ABA-approved law schools in Arkansas—at the state universities in Fayetteville or Little Rock—charge state residents only about $500 annually for tuition and fees. The law schools at West Virginia and Oklahoma universities are only slightly more expensive. All schools charge students from out-of-state twice as much or more.

LEARNING ON YOUR OWN

Cheapest Way to Buy New Books

A number of secondhand book stores, such as the Strand Book Store (at 12th Street and Broadway in New York) sell "reviewers' copies"—books sent free by the publishers to book reviewers for newspapers and magazines and then sold by the reviewers to the stores at half the publishers' price. Selections are limited and many titles are not available in this way. Page proofs, bound together before publication, are even cheaper, often $1.00 each, but they may lack illustrations and contain numerous typographical errors.

Best Way to Track Down a Book That's Hard to Find

The easiest way to obtain a book that is "out of print" or not available in the stores or from the original publisher is by putting an expert to work on finding it. You can probably find one in the Yellow Pages under "Book Dealers—Used and Rare." Make sure of the procedure, though. When your book is found you should be notified of its costs. Only when you've approved the purchase does the dealer acquire it for you. You pay only that agreed-upon purchase fee.

Cheapest Way to Buy Scholarly Books

Check the *Chronicle of Higher Education*, or write to scholarly organizations listed in the *Encyclopedia of Associations* (available in public libraries) to see if a scholarly meeting, conference, or convention is being held nearby—most large cities host several annually. Scholarly books in the appropriate field are usually available at the book exhibits at the conventions with discounts averaging 20 percent. It is normally necessary to register for the meeting, but there are usually low student rates, in some cases as little as $3.00.

Cheapest Book Store

Thrift shops in large cities practically give away books, but there is very little selection. Graduates of a few colleges run volunteer-operated used book stores in large cities (listed in the Yellow Pages) with somewhat larger selections and prices almost as low. Occasionally secondhand book stores simply discard books; the latter are generally available free for the asking, although in some cases they may have to be taken out of garbage cans. In a few areas libraries sell discarded books for low prices. Various book sales organized by charitable groups are advertised in the *New York Times* Sunday Book Review section.

Most Efficient Book Store

Barnes & Noble (18th Street and Fifth Avenue, New York 10003 tel: 212-255-8100) is enormous and orders books. For scholarly books, Basil Blackwell, Broad Street, Oxford, England OX1 3BQ which does much of its business by mail and has an express airmail service, is better.

Cheapest Way to Learn a Foreign Language

In some large cities and suburbs the public school system organizes free or nominally priced evening adult education classes, including classes in the more popular languages. It is usually necessary to be a resident of the city or town involved. Check with the local board of education or the newspapers.

Fastest Way to Learn a Foreign Language

Various language schools, such as Berlitz, have intensive—and expensive—"total immersion" courses, in some cases involving individual tutoring. Some of these use methods devised by the U.S. government for the armed forces or the foreign service. Conversation is emphasized rather than grammatical rules. Details are usually available at public libraries or by contacting the schools themselves.

Free Information about Adult Education

Adults who are interested in pursuing their education, whether to get a degree, to become more proficient at their job, to get a better job, or simply to enrich their lives should get in touch with the Clearinghouse on Adult Education and Life-Long Learning. It has all kinds of information for the adult student.

Call toll-free at 1-800-638-6628, or write, in care of Informatics, Inc., 6011 Executive Boulevard, Rockville, Maryland 20852.

Fastest Way to Get Detailed Reports of Overseas News in English

Listen to foreign broadcasts on a shortwave radio, many of which are in English. The BBC and Deutsche Welle are particularly good. Under certain atmospheric conditions it is possible to get Canadian, Mexican, or West Indian—occasionally even British—domestic programs. The Voice of America also gives detailed foreign commentaries, and those whose native language is not English might appreciate broadcasts in "Special," i.e. slow and simplified, English.

JOBS

Free Job Advice

The Department of Labor publishes a monthly bulletin, *Occupations in Demand at Job Service Of-*

fices, which gives prospective job seekers a good nationwide picture of which jobs are most in demand, and where. The bulletin is available free.

Just write to: U.S. Department of Labor, Employment and Training Administration, Washington, D.C. 20213.

Best Time to Look for a Job

When you've already got one. Employers are much more receptive to job applications from people who are already working and would like to improve their positions.

Fastest Way to Get a Job in an Emergency

Go to a temporary employment agency. Look in the phone directory's Yellow Pages under: "Employment Contractors—Temporary Help." Whether you're a computer operator, a nurse, a file clerk, or a laborer, there's generally a temporary agency that can place you immediately. Most open early. Be there in the morning and they'll usually place you in a job that day, says a New York employment counselor.

Fastest Service by an Employment Agency

Secretaries and typists are in such great demand in the New York area and other large cities that agencies specializing in these occupations probably provide the fastest service. People with typing of 70 or more words per minute are sometimes referred on the same day. The same is true of some temporary employment services for persons with office skills.

Most Efficient Way to Get Information on Summer Jobs with the Government

The Office of Personnel Management will send you, free of charge, a detailed bulletin of summer jobs available with federal government agencies.

These jobs include both ordinary temporary employment and trainee positions that could lead to long-term federal employment later on. The bulletin lists the positions, the qualifications necessary to apply, the general pay range, and explains the procedures the applicant should follow.

For a copy, write to the Washington Area Office, Office of Personnel Management, P.O. Box 52, Washington, D.C. 20044.

Fastest Lead on a Summer Job

One of the great bonanzas for summer job seekers is the roughly 6,000 jobs made available each summer by the concessionaires in the national parks of the United States. There is a wide variety of jobs, from guide to nurse.

A list of the concessionaires who have these jobs available can be obtained, free, from the National Park Service, Washington, D.C. 20240.

Surest Way to Get a Job While Taking Time Off from College

More and more undergraduates are interrupting their studies for a semester or more these days to explore the working world. One of the best ways to find such a job, particularly in a public service field, is through the College Venture Program, a job placement agency specifically geared to students taking time off from their studies. The program, based at Brown University in Providence, Rhode Island, has hundreds of jobs across the country and abroad. Most of the jobs pay a small salary and/or provide room and board. They are in a variety of fields, from publishing to counseling. There may be a small fee for use of the service.

For further information, contact Susan Stroud, Director, College Venture Program, P.O. Box 1838, Brown University, Providence, Rhode Island 02912.

CAREER ADVENTURE

Surest Way to Find Out about Jobs Overseas

In order to get a job overseas you first have to know where the openings are. One of the best ways to get information about openings abroad is to contact International Publications, P.O. Box 29193, Indianapolis, Indiana 46229. For a small fee the company will supply you with information on job openings in a variety of fields throughout the world. International Publications also provides booklets on the best way of going about getting the job you want.

Get a Job Abroad

If you have traveled a great deal and have some leadership experience, you might be interested in becoming a group leader for the Experiment in International Living. Group leaders are primarily responsible for supervising the activities of a group of high school or college age students visiting a particular country in Europe or South America. All leaders must be at least 21 years of age.

For more information, write the Experiment in International Living, Brattleboro, Vermont 05301.

Surest Way to Get a Job in Britain

Americans have traditionally had difficulty finding work overseas, particularly in Europe. However, there is now at least one sure-fire way to find a position in Great Britain. The Community Service Volunteers Program, a London-based private charity organization, places both natives and foreigners in a wide variety of public service jobs throughout England, Wales, Scotland, Northern Ireland, and the Republic of Ireland. The pay is minimal (about $15 per week), but room and board are provided. Virtually all ablebodied, well-intentioned individuals are accepted into the program. There is a placement fee of 50 pounds (about $120) to cover administrative and overhead expenses.

For further information, contact Elinor Tollinton, c/o Community Service Volunteers, 237 Pentonville Road, London NI, England.

Where College Teachers Are Paid Most

If you're a college teacher and feel that you're not getting paid anywhere near what you're worth, you might consider taking off for the land of the Eskimos. The University of Alaska pays its professors higher salaries than any other college in the country. Otherwise, most of the other highest paying universities are in the East. Harvard, Columbia, and the University of Pennsylvania are among those giving out the biggest paychecks to full and associate professors. These three schools, as well as the five other Ivies, however, are traditionally very stingy in paying their untenured assistant professors and lecturers.

Marine Biology

The Cousteau Society works to encourage interest and careers in marine biology through Project Ocean Search (POS). It offers programs and seminars run by people working in and with the sea on a daily basis. And for a "personal experience with the sea" the society offers remote projects where participants have an opportunity to actually observe and experiment with what they've heard presented in lectures on archaeology, anthropology, and marine topics. The program is open to all people over the age of sixteen.

For more information write to: The Cousteau Society, Project Ocean Search, 777 Third Avenue, New York, New York 10017.

Easiest Way to Get Your Name in the Newspaper

Write a letter to the editor of your local *weekly* newspaper complimenting him/her on something that has appeared in the publication, or just say how much you enjoy reading the paper every week. Most weekly newspapers have begun to publish letters-to-the-editor columns and are starved for letters on almost any subject. After your first letter has appeared, you have a better chance at getting others printed—provided they contain nothing slanderous.

Cheapest, Most Effective Way to Advertise

Place your company's name in the telephone directory's Yellow Pages. This one-time placement cost advertises your services and establishes your company's name for one year. Most Yellow Pages directories close their publication four to five months prior to the date of issue (e.g. October closing for March issue). A single line that includes your name, address, and phone number can cost less than $2 a month in regular type (**bold type** costs five times more). As listings are alphabetized, a listing using an "A" would place you at the top of the category advertised. According to a telephone company spokesman, ads can be paid in a lump sum or through monthly payments. (The Reuben H. Donnelly Corporation is the ad agency which handles publication of the Yellow Pages.)

Chapter 9
MONEY MATTERS

BUYING AND SELLING

Free Up-to-date Consumer Information

Each month the *National Consumer Buying Alert* helps give consumers a desperately needed edge in the battle against inflation by keeping track of production and price trends in the vital areas of food, energy, housing, and health care. Its consumer calendar advises readers of the products and services most likely to be on sale in the coming month, pinpointing the best details likely to be available.

Perhaps the best deal of all, however, is the *National Consumer Buying Alert* itself. It's available free each month from the Consumer Information Center, Pueblo, Colorado 81009.

Shoppers Also Can Clip Coupons for Cash

The way to save money with coupons is to clip, save and use every coupon available, not just the ones that show up in the weekly food store ads. That means: the coupons in the magazines, shopping throwaways, on and in packages, and from every other conceivable source. It means using the coupons when you need the items—even preparing menus around them—and not buying anything you ordinarily would not.

One useful time for buying with coupons, whether or not you need the item immediately, is when the local supermarket has it on sale. That sale price plus your cents-off coupon increases your savings.

The refunds are also helpful. A 15¢ stamp is a good investment when it returns a dollar or thereabouts—or if it brings you other coupons for more packages of goods.

You can save as much as $25 a week with coupons, if you devote enough time and energy to saving and using them.

Increased Postage Means Decreased Petrol

With energy costs rising, more and more people will be heeding the Postal Service's adjuration: "Shop by Mail and Save Gas." The U.S. Commerce Department predicts reduced comparison shopping, fewer visits to suburban malls, and greater attention to catalogues, mail and telephone ordering services.

The department also predicts a continuing growth in the sales of generic nontrademarked items as prices climb.

If You Don't Buy Plastic, You'll Probably Pay Less

Whatever it is—hardware, food, soaps, etc.—it probably will cost more when it comes wrapped in plastic than if it's sold loose, or in cardboard or glass containers. Plastic may be more attractive, more hygienic, more convenient, but plastic-bubbled it is made from oil and, therefore, more expensive. The merchandise hanging from hooks in stores is more expensive than the same items purchased loose. (If you even can find them sold that way! Who besides carpenters remembers when nails were sold by the pound?)

How to Make Long-distance Calls for Nothing

More and more businesses are using "800" numbers for long-distance calls from customers and potential customers, and it means they pay for the call, not you. Over a thousand hotels and motels around the country can be reached via 800-323-1776, for example.

Before you make a long distance call to a business firm of any kind, check 800-555-1212 to see if the company you want has an "800" listing.

Cheapest Way to Buy Large Items

For the over 3 million members of the over 1,700 organizations affiliated with the United Buying Service, the cheapest way to make a major purchase is to contact UBS. The member tells the service what it is he/she wants to buy, and UBS then sends a discount certificate for the item in question, good at a dealer in the member's geographical area. These discounts range from 10 to 60 percent off the manufacturer's suggested retail price and cover items such as appliances, furniture, and color television sets. Cars are available at $150 over dealer's cost. If your employer or union is not affiliated with UBS, you might suggest it to them. It could save you, and the other members of your organization, a lot of money.

The toll-free number for UBS (for most of the United States) is 800-223-9855.

Best Time to Ask Your Car Dealer for a Price on Your Trade-in

After he's given you a firm price on the car you plan to buy. In writing. Dealers love to jiggle new car and trade-in prices to make it seem that you're getting a better deal than you really are. If you get a firm cash price from the dealer before talking trade-in, you can compare the price he'd give you on your trade-in with what you could get from a used-car dealer on a straight cash sale, or what you could get by selling your car yourself.

Cheapest Way to Get Real Estate Appraisal

All county tax assesors' offices carry appraisals of real estate on their tax rolls provided by impartial experts who are probably also residents of the area. A visit or call to the tax assessor's office will yield a "tax appraisal" of the property under consideration. This appraisal is not necessarily the market price—it might be 100 percent of the supposed market price at a certain date, or a percentage of it. The office can provide the ratio, and you will have an impartial judgment of the estimated market value of the proposed purchase. Spot market conditions, urgency of sale (or purchase) and other factors—like interest rates—will influence the actual settling price, but the tax appraisal is frequently a valuable tool in evaluation.

Fastest Way to Decide Whether You can Afford a House

There are two guidelines which have most often been recommended by experts in deciding how much you can afford to pay for a house: first, the total price of the house should not be higher than 200 to 250 percent of your family's yearly income. If your family income is at all unstable, you should use the

200 percent figure. The second guideline is based on the cost of the house plus the likely maintenance expenses you would incur as owner, and it suggests that your total housing expenses each month—mortgage payment plus utilities and maintenance—should not exceed 25 percent of your family's monthly income.

Cheapest Way to Sell Your House

Do it yourself and save the average 6 to 7 percent commission. The cost of advertising and of an experienced real estate lawyer—plus a professional appraiser if you feel you need one—will not come anywhere near the cost of the commission.

Remember that repairs and maintenance made in the ninety days before selling your house are considered capital improvements and can be included in the cost of the house for income tax purposes.

Remember also that frequently the little touches—flowers in the rooms, polished floors, and the best bedspreads—can convince a hesitant prospect.

GIFTS

Best Buys

It may not be easy to think of the Post Office as a bargain hunters' mecca but occasionally it comes through. Its sales of undeliverable items are definitely worth watching for. To receive notification of auction dates, write to the Postmaster, Dead Parcel Post Branch, in your nearest big city.

Custom Office sales of unclaimed goods may also yield some fascinating buys. To be on their mailing list, write to the U.S. Customs Service in your nearest port city.

Cheapest Gift

If you receive something in the mail which you

did not order, you are legally entitled to keep it as
a gift.

Best Time to Shop for Christmas Presents

Early January. Just after Christmas it's possible
to find almost anything on sale, and inflation will
certainly boost the prices of most Christmas gifts
by the next December. Give serious consideration
to doing your Christmas shopping in January. You
could save yourself a lot of money.

SAVINGS

Fastest Way to Save for a Treat

The next time you want a small something extra—
a record, book or any not-too-expensive item that's
just a little more than your budget will allow—try
saving your dimes. Every time you get a dime, put
it aside. In no time you'll have your amount—$10,
$15, even $20—and you'll hardly feel a thing.

How to Save $1300 Annually

According to the Federal Highway Administration, a commuter who drives 20 miles to work alone
could save more than $1,300 a year in a four-person
carpool.

For Occasional Use, Rent!

Renting sometimes makes a lot more sense than
buying outright, and practically everything can be
rented—cars, wheelchairs, television sets, dinner
services, and tools. Check the Yellow Pages.

College Campus Copier Cuts Costs

Getting something photocopied is usually simple
enough: libraries, banks, drug and stationery stores
have Xerox or other machines to do the job. But

prices can be as much as 25¢ a page. Best bet is a photocopier machine operation near a college campus: 5¢ or less a page.

Money-making Way to Get Rid of "Junk"

Hold a garage sale. Remember, one person's junk can be someone else's bargain. Just put a classified ad in your local paper, tack up a sign on a nearby tree trunk, assemble the objects you want to get rid of in your garage or driveway along with a comfortable chair for you to sit in, and you'll be all set. You'd be surprised what someone will want to buy. Everything from old furniture to odd-sized picture frames, to used clothes, to—literally—the kitchen sink can be sold at a garage sale. Such sales won't make you rich, but they're better than simply throwing the stuff away, and they're a pleasant way to meet more of your neighbors.

MONEY AND BANKING

Most Efficient Way to Count Cash

Cash is best sorted with all paper money facing the same direction—it's more cheerful face up. It is also easier to notice certain types of counterfeit bills this way, too.

Most Efficient Test for Counterfeit Bills

Fold the bill that you are checking up to the light. If the fibers appear to be *inside* the paper, it's genuine.

Quickest Way to Wire Money

Master Charge maintains an 800 toll-free telephone number that makes it possible to wire money almost anywhere without leaving the house, cashing a check, or sending a telegram. Simply call the toll-free number, obtained locally, and give the name of the recipient, the amount to be sent by wire, and the number of the Master Charge card to be charged.

Cheapest Money Orders

Prices do vary on money orders depending on where you buy them. Savings banks may charge little or nothing to their depositors. Post Office rates and American Express vary according to the amount of money involved. So shop around.

Convenience Can Cost

The "one-stop" bank may not be the one you want. A savings bank, for example, does pay more interest than the commercial bank that offers more services. You then have to order your priorities—time or money.

CHECKS

Protect Your Checks

It may not be possible to cash a check immediately upon receiving it. But you can write on the back of it, "For Deposit Only," with your account number. Don't endorse the check until you are actually at the bank ready to deposit it.

A lost or stolen check, if it is cashed without your signature, may not be your problem. What is your problem is the need to get that check replaced, and it could take considerable time and trouble.

Protect Your Mail

Among the various useful postal services is one aimed at helping to keep thieves away if you're not at home for a couple of days or weeks. Piled-up mail is a tip-off to your absence; the local post office will hold your mail for you if you let them know you plan to be away.

A better bet is, of course, a neighbor who can

bring the mail in for you. While on the premises, he/she also can move window shades and curtains around, turn lights on and off in varying patterns, feed the goldfish and water the plants. Naturally, when the neighbors vacation, you return the favor.

Fastest Way to Write a Check When You're Out of Checks

A check doesn't have to be written on a printed check form supplied by the bank to be legal. If you have to write a check but have run out, just use any ordinary piece of paper—even a napkin would do, if you find yourself short of cash in your favorite restaurant. You should write legibly (or print): the name of the bank in which you have your account, the number of your account if you have it, the name of the person to whom you are writing the check ("Cash" or "Bearer" would do), and a specific demand of the bank to pay him/her the amount in question. It is best to write the amount both in words and figures, as on a standard check. Then sign the paper and you have a valid check.

Most Efficient Way to Write Checks on a Money Fund

Many of the high-interest money funds, sometimes called cash reserve funds, allow you to write checks on your account—but only in amounts of $500 or more. This limit makes the funds unsatisfactory for earning interest on money out of which you'll be paying smaller bills.

The limit can easily be gotten around, however, since most of these funds will allow you to make deposits into your account of amounts starting at $100. If you have small bills to pay, simply write your checking account a check on your money fund of $500, and then write the fund a check for $400, effectively returning most of your $500 withdrawal to earn the fund's high rate of interest. With this procedure you can use these funds to handle much smaller transactions than otherwise, and over the course of a year the extra interest you'll earn—over that you'd earn in a savings account—can be well worth the trouble.

CREDIT

Things You Should Know About Credit

The Equal Credit Opportunity Act prohibits discrimination against an applicant for credit on the basis of these principal factors: age, sex, marital status, race, color, religion, and national origin.

- A creditor may ask how old you are. BUT, your age may not be the basis for an arbitrary decision to deny or decrease credit if you qualify otherwise.
- A creditor may not refuse to consider your retirement income in rating your application.
- A creditor may not close your account just because you reach a certain age, or retire.
- A creditor may not stall you on your application. The law requires that you be notified within thirty days.
- If credit is denied, notice must be in writing, and must give specific reasons or tell you how to obtain such information.

Cheapest Credit Counselors

To learn the name of the nonprofit counseling agency nearest you, write to the National Foundation for Consumer Credit at 1819 H Street NW, Washington, D.C. 20006. They will give you all details about the service and the address of any office in your area.

Three Ways to Build a Credit History

- Open a checking and savings account at your

local bank. This helps to demonstrate your ability to manage your finances.

- Apply for a charge card. Bank charge cards such as Master Charge and Visa are always listed with a credit bureau. Apply where you have your checking and savings accounts.
- A successful record of payment on an installment loan helps to build credit.

Cheapest Time to Straighten Out Your Credit Rating

Within thirty days of being notified of an unfavorable credit report made on you by any credit reporting agency denying you credit, employment, or insurance, you have a right under the Fair Credit Reporting Act to receive a free explanation from that agency of the nature, substance, and in some cases even the source of their negative information about you. If you wait beyond the thirty days, you still have the right to receive the information, but you will probably have to pay a fee to get it. In either case, this right can be valuable to you. If the information the credit agency has about you contains demonstrable inaccuracies, you have the right to have them corrected—and everyone who received the unfavorable report on you must be informed of the corrections by the credit agency. If the agency refuses to make such changes, you have the right to sue.

Fastest Way to Improve Your Credit Rating

Go into bankruptcy! Strange as it sounds, some finance companies seem to prefer the bankrupt with no debts on his slate to the solvent person with many creditors. And they obviously find reassurance in the knowledge that in many cases a bankrupt can't repeat that procedure for another six years. But while some may look with favor on the bankrupt, others take a different view. And remem-

ber, bankruptcy can be listed on your credit record
for fourteen years.

Cheapest Credit Card Protection

Notify the credit card company immediately and
you will not have to pay for any unauthorized
charges if your card is lost or stolen. Some companies have toll-free numbers for you to call.

Even if someone should charge large amounts to
your account before the notification is received,
your liability is still limited to $50 for each credit
card you hold. And the Federal Reserve System
points out that card companies may not collect any
loss at all from you unless they follow certain steps
among which is the provision of a self-addressed
stamped form for you to notify them of your loss.

On electronic fund transfer cards, if you notify
the institution within two business days, your liability remains at $50. Later notification raises your
liability to $500.

Tips for Women and Credit

- The Equal Credit Opportunity Act prohibits lend-
  ers from asking about child-bearing intentions
  or birth control practices.
- The act also prohibits a lender from asking about
  your husband unless you are applying for credit
  jointly with him, or are relying on income or
  payments from him.
- If separated, divorced, or widowed, you are responsible for debts you took on jointly (cosigned)
  with your husband, regardless of court agree-
  ments or settlements.
- The Equal Credit Opportunity Act requires that
  when a husband and wife obtain joint credit it be
  recorded for both under their separate names.
  This provision can be a definite advantage at a
  later date to a housewife with no income of her
  own who needs to find employment and credit at
  the same time.

LOANS AND DEBTS

Cheapest Loan

The cheapest of all loans—apart from the one you get from that rich relative willing to waive the interest—is probably the passbook loan on your savings account. The bank already has your money, so they're risking nothing. They charge a smaller interest on such a loan, and they also pay you interest on the money in deposit. The drawback is, of course, that you can't withdraw any of your savings up to whatever is owed.

A credit union loan, or borrowing against life insurance, can also cut interest costs.

Free Money

Strange as it may seem in this time of soaring interest rates, it *is* possible to get free money—at least for short periods of time. In fact, you probably get some right now if you have a major credit card. With most of these cards, the loans for consumer purchases made on them only begin to be charged interest a month or more after the purchases are registered with the credit card company. The money that you borrowed to finance these purchases is, in essence, loaned to you, for free, for that amount of time. Once that grace period is over, however, you pay for your loan at whopping rates. If you're prompt, you can make good use of this "free money." Not only can you enjoy the benefits of a thirty-day (or longer) interest-free consumer loan, but the money you would have used to pay cash for the purchase can be earning money for you in the meantime, either in your savings account or, better yet, in a cash reserve fund account.

Cheapest Way to Settle a Charge Account Debt

If you can't seem to settle your revolving charge

account bills, you could save money by acquiring a low-interest bank loan in order to pay off that higher-interest charge account.

Advantages of Secondary Mortgage Loans

Many banks offer secondary mortgage loans. Based on the equity in your home you can borrow for home improvements, education, bill consolidation, or other valid reasons, with these advantages:

- No closing costs
- No application fees
- No appraisal fees
- No prepayment penalty

Best Thing to do When You Can't Make Your Payments

Millions of homeowners and other consumers each year find themselves unable to meet one or more financial obligations. Whether it's a mortgage payment, credit card payment, or the payment on their furniture, you may discover that because of some unforeseen financial development or just plain bad judgment you have at least one large bill you simply don't have the money to pay.

One of the most common responses to this situation is to hide from your creditors. You pull in your wagons, stop answering the phone, throw away letters, and generally try to avoid the reality of your debt as long as possible. This is probably the worst thing you can do. Ordinarily, the best thing you can do when you've fallen behind is to contact your creditor. You should explain as honestly as you can how you got into the difficulty, and—most importantly—suggest how you might be able to get out of it. Present your creditor with some kind of plan under which you'll be able to pay off your debt eventually. Remember, in most cases your creditor has no interest in punishing you. He would rather you pay your debt, even if more slowly than originally bargained for, than have to repossess the property involved.

BANKRUPTCY

The Fastest Way to Calculate Candidacy for Bankruptcy

Thinking about filing bankruptcy? Financial planners generally suggest that if you're considering bankruptcy you should estimate your take-home pay for the next three years. Based on this income, if it's doubtful that you'll be capable of paying all your bills and still live reasonably well, bankruptcy makes sense. One study indicated that the average person filing bankruptcy had accumulated debts equaling 9 percent more than his gross annual salary. So bankruptcy may be advisable for an individual with a $15,000-a-year income and $16,350 in debts.

The Most Efficient Way to Retain Possessions During Bankruptcy

A bankrupt can retain ownership of some possessions. Although laws vary from state to state, you can generally keep (1) a portion of your recent wages, (2) at least some of the equity in your house, (3) some of your furniture, (4) all of your clothes, (5) part of your savings in a savings and loan association, and (6) life insurance that designates a spouse or dependent relative as the beneficiary. To take fullest advantage of your bankruptcy proceedings, transfer as many of your nonexempt assets as possible into exempt ones before you file your papers with the U.S. District Court. For instance, you can legally withdraw money from a bank and buy life insurance with it, denoting a child or a spouse as the beneficiary.

The Fastest Way to Reestablish Credit after Bankruptcy

For an individual who has already filed bankruptcy, credit can eventually be reestablished, although the road isn't an easy one. The quickest route is to go to a bank, apply for a small loan, and use a relative or close friend as a cosigner. Then pay back the loan rapidly, thus taking the first step toward reinstating your financial credibility.

SOCIAL SECURITY

Fastest Social Security Answers

Use Teleservice—the special phone number set up to handle any Social Security questions or problems. Everything from applying for benefits to reporting a lost or stolen check can be handled by phone now. To find your Teleservice phone number, check in the phone directory under Social Security Administration (U.S. Government). Teleservice is available Monday through Friday—with some offices also having lines open evenings and Saturdays.

Quickest Way to Get Social Security

Sometimes a type of "Social Security" benefit may be obtained before the proposed recipient is 65 years of age. Disabled persons without extra income from securities or unemployment benefits of any kind may apply for "Supplemental Security Income." If, for example, an illness or injury has incapacitated you for a period of time and, in the opinion of a physician, will keep you incapacitated for a period of a year or more, Social Security benefits may be paid to you on a monthly basis. Persons who have earned less than a stipulated figure—it was $3,700 for 1980—for two years or more for reasons beyond their control (like physical injury or personality difficulties) are sometimes eligible too. Information about this portion of the "negative income tax" is available through a visit to the local Social Security Office, which is listed under "Health, Education, and Welfare" in the telephone directory in the section devoted to U. S. Government.

Ask and You Shall Receive

You may have to wait on a long line, but the surest way of obtaining deserved governmental assistance is by going to the nearest appropriate office and asking for it. You may not know what you are entitled to—as a veteran, a would-be vocational or college student, a citizen or a senior citizen, or a small business man. Get there when the office opens; it cuts down on your waiting time. And, of course, bring along all documents relative to whatever your particular immediate interest is.

Easiest Way to Deposit Monthly Government Checks

Direct deposit. The government encourages the recipients of all recurring government checks to deposit them directly into a financial institution. These federal payments include: Social Security Benefits, Supplemental Security Income, Civil Service Retirement Benefits, Federal Railroad Retirement Benefits, Veterans Administration Compensation, and Pension Payments.

Advantages of direct deposit are:

- You save a special trip to the bank to deposit your check.
- Your money goes to work for you promptly.
- It eliminates worry about the check being lost or stolen.
- Your check is automatically deposited for you if you are away on business or vacation, or are ill.

- The service is free.
- You can arrange with your bank to transfer a portion of your check each month from checking to savings.

You can obtain the appropriate form from your bank, complete it, and return it to the bank. They will do the rest.

HEALTH INSURANCE

Fastest "Group" Health Insurance

Many members of fraternal, social, or religious organizations are insured as a group at reduced rates. Coverage can be boon to the self-employed or sporadically employed individual who has no on-the-job protection and doesn't want to pay higher individual rates.

Fastest "Group" Health Insurance

You and two or three others claiming to be your co-workers in a "small business" (no other proof is necessary) may qualify for lower group rates from some of the large medical insurers. All you need to do is phone a few and find out what the qualifications are at each company.

LIFE INSURANCE

Cheapest Life Insurance

Savings bank life insurance is the cheapest available, with term insurance following. Straight life isn't really a way of saving money; putting the premiums into a bank is better.

Least Expensive Life Insurance

In terms of cash dollars paid for premiums, "term" insurance is the lowest in price of any life coverage. Term insurance is the "no-frills" of the underwriting business; the insured person pays a monthly or other periodic premium based on life expectancy in the company's actuarial tables and age at inception of plan and during its existence. The death benefit is a fixed sum agreed in advance. Term insurance has no investment or cash withdrawal value except for the exact terms of the written policy and is usually written for short periods of time.

Most Efficient Insurance Investment

The least expensive—but not necessarily cheapest investment in life insurance—is a policy placed at or near birth of a child (usually within the first year of life). When the child reaches the age of twenty-one, the policy can become a "jumping juvenile" life insurance policy, in which both face value and cash withdrawal value of the policy are increased automatically in $1,000 increments without an increase in premiums. Premiums on the life of a newborn child are low. In addition, depending on the nature of the policy, it can be useful collateral for a loan for college or other training. Persons at age twenty-one who take over ownership of a policy provided for them by a farsighted relative or benefactor may be able to exercise one or more of several investment options with the existing policy, including a modest lifetime income.

Most Efficient Way to Shop for Life Insurance

Since comparative "values" in life insurance are difficult (perhaps impossible) for the potential customer to calculate, the Federal Trade Commission has encouraged development of independent rating or evaluation services that may offer you useful measuring tools to help decide which life insurance plan is most suitable for your investment and protection objectives. An easy—though still new and controversial—index is called "The Linton Yield"

(SIC), and provides a numbered grading system to suggest the investment desirability of various plans. Information about the "yield" will be published in selected reporting media like *Consumer Reports, Journal of Commerce,* and the *New York Times*.

Best Insurance Payment Schedule

Paying insurance annually instead of monthly or quarterly saves money. Paying in advance, two years instead of one, may lead to a discount.

All it takes is money.

OTHER INSURANCE

When Insurance Isn't Doing the Job

Inflation creates other problems besides increased prices on food, gasoline, personal services, and the like. The value of a home may have increased so much that an insurance policy (which probably was never adequate in the first place) must be adjusted upward. The replacement costs of furnishings, clothing, and other items in the home may now be way out of line.

Also out of line may be personal liability insurance in this day of high medical costs.

Toughest part of the problem, of course, is that increased insurance means increased premiums—inflation feeding on itself.

Quickest Way to Insure an Object of Value

If you have an established relationship with an insurance broker, you can insure a new purchase of, say, a fur coat simply by telephoning your broker to ask for a "binder" on insurance for the object. This particular oral contract is valid from the moment of the conversation but must be followed in a stipulated period of time—often three days—by a formal contract, payment of premium, and issuance of a written policy. Latitude and restriction on this type of insurance activity is regulated by individual state agencies.

Government (not GI) Insurance

A U.S. government policy against loss from burglary or robbery may be obtained in some states if no private company will give you the policy. Insurance is up to $10,000, and premiums vary from $60 to more a year.

For information, write Federal Crime Insurance, P.O. Box 41033, Washington, D.C. 10014.

Surest Way to Settle an Insurance Claim

Don't settle with a claims agent from the company immediately unless you are positive you're collecting on your total loss to the extent possible under your policy.

To be sure of that, start work on an insurance claim for fire or theft now—by having lists and bills of the more important items safely stowed away somewhere along with photographs. The company will want to know such things as replacement value, place of purchase or gift from whom, depreciation, and net value.

Your report to the police may be helpful, as will the fire department's report.

The reason for not settling immediately is that in the anguish of the moment you may forget some important lost item(s), even with the lists.

INVESTING

Fastest Way to Take Advantage of Today's High Interest Rates

Inflation has given savings a bad name. There's no way for you as a small saver to get ahead of inflation by putting your money in a bank or savings-and-loan institution, where the interest rates given to savers are well below the rise in the cost of living. One place where you can get a rate that approaches, and at times even beats, the rate of inflation, however, is in the so-called money market or cash reserve funds. Money in these funds is invested in short-term money market securities, usually only available to large investors in denominations of $100,000 or more. Needless to say, the interest rates available are much higher than those available at your local bank. By pooling the usually smaller amounts deposited by their investors, the funds can take advantage of these high rates and pass most of that advantage along to their clients. Many of these funds will open an account for you for only $1,000, and many have a kind of checking service available whereby you can write a check on your fund account for any amount (up to the balance in the account, of course) over $500. Interest rates offered by these funds vary from fund to fund and week to week, so check before you invest.

Easiest Way to Open a Swiss Franc Bank Account

The Swiss franc has long been a haven for foreigners worried about the reliability of their own currency. In recent years this has included large numbers of Americans. Unfortunately, it is impossible to open a Swiss franc (or other foreign currency) bank account in the United States. The most common approach for Americans interested in such an account has been to open one by mail with a bank in Switzerland. That tends to be a fairly long procedure. Mail between this country and Switzerland is erratic and expensive. And there are other disadvantages. Your correspondent at the Swiss bank, who will write in English, may not write it very well, and confusion can arise. In addition, most banks in Switzerland require fairly large initial deposits from foreign customers.

These problems can be avoided by opening your Swiss franc account with a Swiss bank in the Bahamas, rather than in Switzerland. The Bank Leu International Ltd. offers both regular and savings accounts, denominated in Swiss francs, to American customers. The mail between here and the Bahamas tends to be somewhat faster than between here and Switzerland, your correspondent is likely to be a native English-speaker, and accounts may be opened with small amounts. For those interested in other aspects of the fabled Swiss bank account, it should be noted that the Bahamas have a bank secrecy law similar to that of Switzerland.

GOLD

Most Efficient Way to Invest in Gold

There are a number of ways to invest in gold, from the purchase of bullion itself to heavily margined gold options. Bullion, however, is relatively difficult to store and relatively easy to steal, and gold options are extremely risky. Gold can be bought and stored for you in a Swiss bank, but this is a fairly complicated procedure, involving large amounts of money and the opening of a foreign bank account.

By investing in gold jewelry or gold coins, the average investor starts at a great disadvantage—you have to buy at retail and sell at wholesale. The mark-ups on both jewelry and coins can be enormous. Besides, such specialized investments require great expertise, for the risk of counterfeits is high.

All in all, then, the most efficient gold investment currently available—the one with the fewest extraneous risks combined with the greatest safety and ease—is a gold deposit certificate, issued by the international banking firm of Deak and Company and marketed through their offices and those of the brokerage firm of Shearson Hayden Stone, Inc., throughout the United States. Certificates can be purchased in any amount from $2,500 on up. It's as easy as buying a money order.

Each certificate represents a specific interest in the appropriate amount of gold bullion, stored in the name of Deak and Company with a bank in Zurich, Switzerland. The gold (and the investor's interest in it) is protected against any possible failure of either Deak and Company or the Swiss bank and is fully insured against theft or damage. Not only is the gold itself insured, but the certificate is registered in your name, so that even if a thief were to steal the certificate he couldn't negotiate it. The gold is bought and sold at the "spot price" in Zurich, a published free market price, and commission and storage fees are as low as the ordinary investor can find anywhere. If you wish, you can actually have the gold bullion represented by the certificate delivered to you.

Cheapest Gold Coin

Many people choose to invest in gold by having gold coins. While this is not the most efficient way to invest in gold, the coins do have some advantages: they're handy, easy to transport, their gold content is immediately recognizable, and they are therefore easily bought and sold. Currently, the most popular bullion coins (that is, coins which are bought purely for the gold they contain rather than for any numismatic value) are the South African Krugerrand and the new Canadian Maple Leaf. Each of these contains approximately one ounce of gold. The great popularity of these coins comes largely from heavy advertising by the governments who mint them.

When buying a bullion coin, however, the most important factor for an investor should be the premium on the coin. The premium is the amount over and above the pure gold value of the coin which is charged for it by the dealer. It is, of course, the premium which provides the dealer's profit. And from the investor's point of view, the smaller the premium, the cheaper the gold. Premiums fluctuate, and compared to most gold coins, the popular Kruggerrand and Maple Leafs have had fairly low premiums, but there is another bullion coin whose premium has generally been even lower—the Austria 100 Crowns. As easily bought and sold as either of the others, the 100 Crowns consistently low premium makes it the "cheapest" gold bullion coin available. Recently the Mexican government has been marketing a series of their own low premium coins in this country, but the track record of the Austrian coin is still the best.

Fastest Way to Buy Gold Coins

Pick up a phone. The First National Bank of Chicago gold desk will sell you one or more gold bullion coins over the phone any hour of the business day. Just call their toll-free number, 800-621-4156, and they'll quote you a firm price, including the cost of postage and insurance to mail the coin(s) to your home, and the deal can be concluded then and there. You simply send them a check for the agreed-upon price and they send you the coin(s). When you want to sell the coin, all you have to do is call again, agree on a price, and mail them the coin.

STOCKS

Fastest Way to Get Stock Market Reports

In some cities it is possible to get this information by calling a number available in your telephone book. Downtown districts of large cities are full of brokerage houses, some with ticker tape visible to the general public and/or Dow Jones averages posted in the windows. In large cities frequent reports may be heard on "all news" radio stations.

Free High-Priced Stock Market Advice

Many stock market investors part with hundreds (even thousands) of dollars each year for invest-

ment advisory services such as Moody's or the Value
Line Investment Survey. The Value Line Survey,
for example, charges $295 a year for its stock
market service and another $300 for its convert-
ibles and options advice. Yet many of these services
are available—free—at public libraries.

Safest Way to Keep Stocks and Bonds

Register stocks and bonds in your own name
wherever possible; lost or stolen, they cannot be
negotiated without your signature. Municipal bonds
issued to "bearer" are numbered, and you should
keep a list of those numbers some place other than
where you keep the bonds.

The bonds themselves should be kept in a safety-
deposit box, not at your broker's office or in your
home. Safety-deposit boxes are also subject to
looting, as headlines attest, but they are considerably more secure than anything else around.

Cheapest Way to Invest in a Number of Stocks

Most investors believe in the old adage, "Don't
put all your eggs in one basket." They would rather
invest in a large number of stocks than put all
their money on one or two companies. Buying several good stocks, rather than one, is recommended
by most investment counselors as a way of hedging
your bet.

The trouble is that most small investors don't
have enough money to invest in a lot of stocks.
They fear, rightly, that they'd be spreading themselves too thin and subjecting themselves to too
many commissions. A small investor, after all, has
to pay a commission every time any of the stock is
bought or sold; and purchases of less than 100
shares at a time, known as odd-lots, are subject to
especially high commissions. Besides, the odds
against a small, amateur investor picking fifteen
or twenty good stocks are incredibly high. So what
is the small investor who wants to diversify to do?

The best answer is to buy shares in a mutual
fund. Mutual funds invest in large numbers of
stocks and then sell shares, representing fractions
of the combined asset values of all the stocks in
their portfolio, to the public. The stocks are chosen
by professional investment managers, who then keep
track of them, buying and selling when the time
seems right. But for the purchaser of the mutual
fund's shares it's a simple, one-time purchase.
Instant diversity and professional management to
boot.

Another big plus for the mutual fund investor is
not being subjected to high, small-investor commissions every time a stock in the fund's overall portfolio is bought or sold. Instead, much smaller fees,
covering transaction costs and management payments, are subtracted from the gross asset value of
the fund. All you pay directly are the one-time buy
and sell commissions when you buy and sell the
shares of the mutual fund itself—and, if you choose
one of the so-called no-load funds, you don't even
have to pay a commission when you buy!

Up-to-date price quotations on many of these funds
are available on the stock pages of most major
newspapers every weekday. A particularly compre-
hensive list can be found in the *Wall Street Journal*.

Cheapest Leverage on a Stock

Leverage is the key to high percentage capital
gains in the stock market. With leverage you can
control more stock than could be purchased with
the amount of money you have available, and therefore can get a higher percentage of increase in the
price of the stock itself.

There are several ways to get leverage. The most
common is (or used to be) margin. If you buy stock
"on margin" you borrow money from your broker
to enable you to buy more stock than you could
afford with your own capital. Margin buying has

some serious disadvantages, however. The amount of margin you can get is restricted by law, the interest rates charged are high, and if the stock goes down before it goes up you're always subject to a call from your broker (known as a "margin call") demanding that you invest more money or he'll sell the stock.

Most of these disadvantages can be eliminated, however, through the use of call options. Instead of buying stock, you buy a "call" on 100 shares of the stock. This call assures you of the right to buy the stock, at a specified price, any time up to a set date in the future. A call is, of course, much less expensive than the stock itself; and if you pick a call on a stock that goes up in price, your percentage gain on your actual investment can be huge. That's leverage.

For example, say Stock X is selling at $18 a share. You buy a call option which gives you the right to purchase that stock at $20 a share any time in the next two months. The call might cost you $2. If the stock goes up to $24 within the allotted time, the owners of the stock will have a profit of $6, or 33⅓ percent on their investment. Your call option, however, would have gone up to at least its break-even point of $4. (That's its break-even point, ignoring commissions for the purpose of example, because the option gives you the right to purchase the stock at $20, $4 below the present price of the stock.) The profit on the call option, then, is 100%.

If the stock goes up further, the leverage is even more significant. Say the stock goes up to $36 a share, a profit of 100 percent for the stock's owners. With the stock worth $36 a share, your call might easily sell at its break-even point of $16—an incredible 700 percent profit on your original investment!

There are, however, some disadvantages to options. First of all, they're time limited. Most are good for less than a year, and once the time limit is passed, they're worthless. It's important to remember that leverage works both ways. It offers an opportunity for large percentage gains, but it also offers an opportunity for large percentage losses.

Another disadvantage to options is that they're only available on some stocks. If you're interested in a call option on a given stock, check with a broker. He or she can tell you whether options are available on it and fill you in on other things you need to know about investing in options.

Cheapest Leverage on a Falling Stock

To make money on a falling stock, leverage is available through the purchase of a "put option." But options work the same way as call options (see above), only in reverse. They give you the right to *sell* a given stock at a certain price by a certain date. Consequently, once the stock has reached the break-even point, the put option increases in value as the stock goes down.

Fastest Way to Make Money on a Falling Stock

Sell short. Selling means to sell a stock you don't own, and it's perfectly legal. What you actually do is borrow the stock from your broker, sell it just as you would any other stock, at the prevailing price, in the expectation that the price of the stock is going to go down. When (and, of course, *if*) it does, you can buy it back at the new, lower price, return the stock to the broker and pocket the difference— less commissions and taxes—as your profit. If the stock price goes up, however, the stock's true owner may demand it back and you'll have to pay the new, higher price in order to buy the shares to return to him. In that case, the difference between the price at which you sold and the price at which you later bought, *plus* commissions and any applicable taxes, will be your loss.

Cheapest Way to Enter the Bureau of Land Management's Oil and Gas Lottery

Advertisements in many publications invite readers to enter the "Government's Oil and Gas Lotteries." The "lotteries" in question are used by the government to distribute leases on certain government lands, mostly in western states, on which previous oil and gas leases have expired. These lotteries are held by the appropriate state offices of the Bureau of Land Management, but the advertisements are not run by the BLM or by any other governmental agency. They are placed by various "filing services" which will enter you in one or more of these lotteries in return for a fee, over and above the $10 filing fee required by the BLM itself. All that's necessary for any citizen to enter one of the lotteries is to submit the $10 entry card (Form 3112-I), which is available free from any BLM state office which conducts a lottery. (These include California, Colorado, Idaho, Montana, Nevada, New Mexico, Utah, and Wyoming.) The U.S. Department of the Interior warns, however, that most lands put up for re-leasing in these lotteries are all but worthless, and that in order to keep such leases once you've "won" you'll be required to pay a rental fee of $1 per acre within fifteen days of being awarded the lease. (Some filing services offer to loan you this rental.) For further information, write for the booklet, *Can You Really Strike It Rich in the Government Oil and Gas Lottery?:* Consumer Information Center, Pueblo, Colorado 8)09.

In fact, according to some investment advisors, one of the few good reasons for participating in such an "investment opportunity" at all is to get a possible tax deduction.

Chapter 10
LAW

LEASES

The Most Efficient Lease

A good rental agreement should include the following elements:

— The length of the lease: when does it stop and start?
— The exact residence (e.g., 841 East Wabash Street).
— The monthly rent.
— How it is to be paid (e.g., on the fifteenth of each month?)
— Various accoutrements included in the rent (tennis courts, laundry room, parking space, swimming pool).

— The party responsible for repairs and maintenance.
— Whether the premises may be sublet to another person.

Most Efficient Way to Break a Lease

Amicably. Talk it over with your landlord, who may be willing to let you out of your lease without a penalty particularly in these times of limited housing construction. If you and your landlord agree, there is no need to change the legal document. Still, it might be better, as in all legal matters, to get it in writing, just in case your landlord's tempted to change his/her mind.

CONSUMER RIGHTS

The Fastest Consumer Complaint Process

If you've bought defective merchandise, proceed through the following steps to rectify the situation:

— Take your complaint to the store that sold you the item;
— Write or call the customer-relations department of the manufacturer;
— Write directly to the company's president—who is listed in *Moody's Industrial Manual*, available in most libraries;
— Mail carbon copies of your letter to consumer protection societies like the Better Business Bureau and Consumers Union;
— Contact the local newspaper or TV station and tell them your complaint;
— As a final resort, take your complaint to Small Claims Court.

Fastest Way to Reach Your Congressional Representative

Want to let your congressperson or senator know

what you think? The quickest way to let them know
is to call their office. All Capitol offices can be
reached through the Capitol Switchboard: 202-
224-3121.

The Most Efficient Legal Way to Divest Your-self of a "Lemon"

Whenever most people buy a new car, they worry
at least a little about having purchased a "lemon."
If you're extremely unhappy with the automobile
you've bought, follow these procedures: (a) ask that
all defects be repaired by the auto agency and keep
an accurate record of when the car was returned
for repairs and the outcome; (b) if the results are
unsatisfactory and the dealer refuses to totally reimburse you for the car, leave the car on the lot,
with a list of the defects attached to the windshield;
before you leave the premises, take the license plates
with you; (c) mail the dealer a notarized letter,
carefully listing your complaints; in the letter, also
state that you have renounced your acceptance of
the car and insist on a full refund; (d) notify your
bank or other lending institution of your situation;
the bank actually holds title to the car. Caution:
Also be sure to check your loan agreement to determine that you don't have any residual obligations to the bank under it.

Fastest Way to Check a Product's Safety

Are you wondering whether a toy you're thinking of buying for your children is safe? Do you
want to check on a rumor about the dangers of a
food additive? The Consumer Product Safety Commission monitors all product safety warnings and
keeps track of all recall orders. They're a treasure
trove of information about what is safe and what
isn't—and what you can do about it. If you have a
question about any product, just call their hot line:
800-638-8326, on any business day.

LAWYERS AND LAWSUITS

Create an Advice Network

Advice professionals can include more than their special knowledge. A lawyer can recommend a good accountant, and either one can recommend a good insurance agent. Use the contacts you trust to lead to others.

Fastest Way to Find a Lawyer

To find a lawyer quickly, call the local county bar association, which will provide you with the name of a lawyer from its referral network. The bar association will make an initial appointment with the attorney for you, which will usually last thirty minutes and cost a nominal fee. If you are not satisfied with the lawyer, you are not obligated to hire him. You can determine the background of any attorney by looking in *The Martindale-Hubbell Lawyer's Dictionary*, which is available in most libraries. This reference book lists all lawyers in the country, their age, the law school they attended, how long they have been practicing, their specialties and types of clients, their financial standing, and their rating with fellow layers.

The Most Efficient Court System

A small claims court is a limited-jurisdiction court that handles relatively minor matters, like contract disputes and arguments between tenants and landlords. To file a small claims suit, go to the office of the clerk of the court and fill out the appropriate forms. If you're suing a store or a business, you need to find out its legal name from official records in the county clerk's office. A fee of from $5 to $15 is required and a court date will usually be designated at that time.

The Cheapest Way to Avoid High Legal Fees

Legal insurance is quickly becoming more accessible, and it offers the best protection against exorbitant legal costs. For a premium of $50 to $200 per year, you'll be entitled to a specified number of meetings with an attorney to discuss issues like wills and credit problems. Just as important, the insurance also covers legal fees for civil and criminal trials.

The Cheapest Lawyer

Individuals who cannot afford to hire an attorney should contact the Legal Aid Society, which has offices in almost every major city in the United States. Legal Aid will handle most types of cases at no charge if the person (a) owns no property, stocks, or bonds, (b) has only a nominal weekly salary, and (c) has only a small amount of money in a savings account.

For uncontested divorce cases, no matter what your income or property holdings, contact agencies like the Wave Project in California or Divorce Yourself in New York. For less than $100, these services will help you fill out the necessary divorce papers.

Fastest Compensation for Incompetent Legal Services

If you are displeased with a lawyer's services, file a formal complaint with the local bar association. Many associations sponsor special funds to reimburse individuals for money or property lost because of unscrupulous or incompetent actions of attorneys.

The Cheapest Legal Arrangement

If you're unable to pay your legal fees all at once, you should ask your lawyer to arrange a monthly payment schedule. Many bar associations now suggest that their lawyers be willing to accept promissory notes from clients. These notes are often turned over to banks, which arrange for the payment of the debts.

The Cheapest Contingency Fee

Contingency fees are used primarily in negligence lawsuits, where one person is seeking monetary damages from another, as in an auto accident. Under this system, if you win the case, your lawyer receives a percentage of your settlement. If you lose, your lawyer gets nothing, handling your case without a fee. When you find a lawyer willing to work for a contingency fee, bargain. Although an attorney may demand a percentage as high as 60 percent, some will work for as little as 25 percent.

The Fastest Path to Justice

Citizens' arrests have a long tradition and are an instant way to start the justice process. But they require some care and knowledge on your part. First, be reasonably certain that the person you arrest has actually committed a crime; if he's innocent, he can bring criminal charges of unlawful arrest against you. Also, in some states, you can only make a citizen's arrest of an individual who has committed a felony; if you arrest someone for a misdemeanor, he can later charge you with false arrest.

ENDING A MARRIAGE

The Fastest Way to Reach an Alimony Settlement

After a divorce, rather than arranging for monthly alimony payments for an indefinite period of time, it is often more advantageous to agree to a single, lump-sum settlement. This arrangement (which must be reached before the divorce decree) places a

clear finish to the marriage and requires no further contact between the parties. Wives, if they are
the recipients of the alimony, often feel most comfortable with a lump-sum payment, since it erases
their concern over whether their ex-husband's salary in the future will decrease, resulting in a de-
cline in their own monthly income. Husbands, when
they are paying the alimony, often appreciate the
lump-sum, too, happy to end their financial obligation all at once, while aware that if their salary
rises in the upcoming years, they obviously won't
have to increase payments to an ex-wife.

The Fastest Wedding Dissolution

A quicker, and less complicated, option to divorce
is an *annulment*, which "voids" a marriage, and
relegates it to a status as though it had never ex-
isted. There are many legal grounds for an annulment, including: underage, sexual impotence, lack
of "true consent" (for example, did the couple marry
on a whim, without serious intention of forming a
lasting relationship?), and fraud (for example, did
one of the marriage partners hide information from
the other, like a history of mental illness or serious
sickness?).

ESTATE PLANNING AND WILLS

Most Important Considerations in Estate Planning

- Proper management of assets during your lifetime, with maximum tax advantages.
- Adequate liquid assets to meet death taxes and
  administrative costs.
- Arrangement of assets in a way best designed to
  assure their most efficient use for your beneficiaries.
- Minimization of tax liability on the individual's
  estate after death.

The Most Efficient Will

For most people a will does not need to be complicated. It only must specify the following four points: (a) the beneficiaries of all money and property; (b) the amount allotted to each beneficiary; (c) the time at which each beneficiary is to receive his or her portion; and (d) the person who is to supervise the distribution of the estate.

Cheapest Power of Attorney

An attorney-in-fact—the person to whom you give your power of attorney—does not have to be a lawyer and in fact seldom is. Using a competent and trusted family member will save expensive lawyer's fees and assure that your personal affairs receive careful attention. But once you are ready to resume control, be sure that the power of attorney is eliminated.

Matters to Include in a Letter of Instruction

In addition to your will, a Letter of Instruction to your family will help them settle your affairs. Make sure that a responsible person knows where to find the letter at all times. It should include:

- Instructions for funeral arrangements.
- A list of those people to be notified about your death, including relatives, friends, employer, and lawyer.
- Provisions and locations of life insurance policies.
- Location of savings and checking accounts, bank books, stocks and bonds, and other securities. Keep your list up to date.
- Location of all personal documents such as your will, birth certificate, and any other papers of importance.
- Location of income tax returns for the past five years.
- Location of safety-deposit box and key.

- A list of loans together with all relevant information.
- A list of accounts receivable, giving specifics.
- A list of items too small to be mentioned in your will that you want to distribute—and to whom you want them to go.

The Fastest Way to Update a Will

A will probably needs to be changed upon a marriage or divorce; the death of a beneficiary or a witness; the birth of a child; or the purchase or sale of property, a business, or other assets. The simplest way to modify a will is by adjoining a codicil to it. A codicil is a document containing amendments or additions to a will. Never cross out outdated clauses of an original will. As the years pass, many codicils can be added to a single will. (Each codicil must be executed with the same formality as the original will.)

The Most Efficient Place to Keep a Will

Although a safety-deposit box may seem the most logical place to keep your will, it's actually a bad choice, unless the box is in your spouse's name so he/she has access to it. Boxes are sealed upon death, and your surviving relatives won't be able to get into the vault immediately to find your will if the box is registered under your name. A court order will be necessary to obtain the will under these circumstances, which could take several weeks. Consider his-or-her safety-deposit boxes, with her will in his box and vice versa.

The Most Efficient Way to Make Bequests

When making out your will, it is wise to make most or all of your bequests in percentages of the net value of your estate—for example, 80 percent to your wife and 20 percent to charity. Specifying dollar amounts can cause problems. For instance, let's say that when your will is prepared, your

estate is worth $100,000 and your will stipulates
that $30,000 should go to charity and the rest to your
wife. If at the time of your death the estate has
diminished in value to $50,000, your wife will only
receive $20,000 after the charity is given its clearly
defined share. To protect your wife, you should
specify a particular percentage that you want your
spouse to receive.

The Most Efficient Distribution of Large Monetary Gifts

When you decide to leave money to a minor—or
to anyone else you feel may be incapable of managing
the money well in one lump sum—your best option
is to place that money in a trust to be activated
upon your death. The recipient will be given a portion of this money each month rather than all of it
at once.

Six Reasons to Consider Establishing a Trust

* Protection of your beneficiaries against their own
  inadequacies—youth, bad judgment, or lack of
  management experience, for example. A trust provides experienced, professional management of
  assets.
* Controlled distribution of your property. A trust
  can provide for a regular income for your spouse
  and/or children.
* Provision for unequal needs: a younger child's
  education, for example, or a dependent's continuing illness may be provided for through a trust
  that permits the trustee to make adjustments as
  necessary.
* Substantial federal estate and state inheritance
  tax savings.
* Income tax savings, if beneficiaries' incomes are
  high.
* Preservation of property intact where that is considered desirable.

Chapter 11
TAXES

THINKING AHEAD

The Most Efficient College-Education Fund

For tax purposes, you should consider either a
custodial savings account or a short-term trust to
finance your child's college expenses. However, you
can lose a portion of your tax savings under these
plans if your youngster is not still a dependent
when the funds are paid out. At that time, if you
fail to contribute over half of a child's cost of living
during the college years, you'll lose the $1,000
dependency exemption each year. The loss of a
$4,000 exemption over four years could defeat the
tax advantages that an education fund can offer.

The Fastest Way to Prepare for Retirement

If you're in business for yourself you can now build up your own tax-free retirement fund, called the Keogh Plan. You can set aside at least 15 percent of your income, not to exceed $1,500 in most cases. Employees not covered by a pension plan can start their own Individual Retirement Plan, with the same $1,500 ceiling.

The Most Efficient Way to Reduce Estate Taxes

You can reduce estate taxes by giving away some of your assets while you're alive. If they do not belong to you upon your death, your estate won't be taxed for them. According to law, you can give up to $3,000 per person per year to as many individuals as you wish for as many years as you desire. Any gift in excess of $3,000 per person per year must be reported to the government on a gift tax return. The tax code was amended in 1976 to provide for a unified treatment for gifts and transfers at death. Beginning in 1981, $118,000 of all such transfers will be exempt from gift-estate taxes.

Most Efficient Bonds to Save Estate Taxes

Elderly people with substantial assets in their estate should consider buying so-called "flower bonds." Bought at a discount from par, these bonds can be turned in at full face value to pay estate taxes. Otherwise, the return on your investment is low.

Cheapest Large City for Taxes

Houston, Texas, which has no zoning laws, is approximately 20 percent cheaper for after-tax income from the same salary than New York City. There is no city income or sales tax, and there is no evidence that public services are inferior. Public

employees receive much lower salaries and benefits
than their counterparts in the Northeast.

PREPARING YOUR TAXES

The Cheapest Way to Get Tax Information

The IRS sponsors its own Taxpayer Service Division, which answers questions about tax problems
without charge over its toll-free telephone lines.
See the phone book for your own local IRS phone
number. Inquiries can also be directed to IRS employees in person at one of the IRS's one thousand
offices throughout the United States.

The Most Efficient Tax Information for Deaf Taxpayers

Deaf people obviously can't take advantage of the
IRS's normal telephone inquiry service. But for those
deaf individuals with teletypewriters or TV phones,
the IRS provides a toll-free telephone service to
answer tax-return inquiries. Call 800-482-4732 (in
Indiana, 800-382-4059) on any weekday.

The Most Efficient Tax Information for the Aged

The special tax situations and problems of senior
citizens are best understood by two senior citizen
groups that can answer almost any tax question.
One of them, the American Association of Retired
Persons (215 Long Beach Boulevard, Long Beach,
CA 90802) has its own Tax Aide service, with local
chapters in most areas of the country. The other
organization is the National Council of Senior Citizens (1511 K Street NW, Washington, D.C. 20005).

The Fastest Way to Reduce the Accountant's Bite

Yes, tax accountants are charging more and more
these days. But their rising fees won't seem quite

as painful when you deduct them on your income taxes. And it's all legal.

The Most Efficient Way to Find a Tax Preparer

If you want to hire a professional tax consultant, Certified Public Accountants (CPAs) certainly have the training to handle the task. However, even an individual who's not a CPA may still be qualified. You should determine his/her abilities through the following question: (1) does the consultant practice accountancy year-round or only during tax season? (2) has the consultant completed a formal tax training course? (3) does he or she belong to any professional accounting organizations? (4) does he practice before the IRS?

The Cheapest Tax Preparers

The IRS will prepare tax returns for individuals who can't or won't do it themselves. In 1980, local IRS walk-in offices prepared over a million returns— for free. No matter how simple or complicated a return may be, IRS employees are obligated to help.

The Fastest Way to Avoid Tax Preparation Fraud

There are many incompetent and even fraudulent tax preparers around. You can avoid being "ripped off" by adhering to the following guidelines: (1) be cautious of a preparer who assures you of a refund even before studying your particular situation; (2) refrain from using a preparer who urges that your refund be sent directly to his or her office; (3) never sign a blank tax return or one that is written in pencil (that can be altered later).

The Most Efficient Time to Itemize

Millions of taxpayers cheat themselves out of money each year when they claim the standard deduction rather than itemizing. As a general rule,

you will benefit from itemizing under any of the
following circumstances:

— You own a home and pay interest and taxes on
  it.
— You have incurred large uninsured medical costs.
— You pay alimony.
— You have suffered major uninsured casualty
  losses.
— You have made large contributions to charity.

The Fastest Tax Reduction Through Income Scrutinizing

Not all income is subject to federal taxes, and
thus need not be included as income on your tax
forms. Examples include: gifts, inheritance, life
insurance benefits, living expenses paid by an
insurance company while a home is being repaired,
certain dividends, Social Security benefits, a divorce
settlement paid in one lump sum, interest on municipal bonds, and scholarships and fellowships.

END-OF-THE-YEAR STRATEGY

The Most Efficient Verification of Check Dates

If you pay bills on December 31, you can't necessarily deduct them on the tax return for that out-
going year. IRS policy states that the date of *delivery*
of the check is usually the factor determining which
year a deduction is valid. Those late-year checks,
then, should be mailed a few days before year's
end.

The Most Efficient End-of-the-Year Tax Strategy

Taxes can be reduced by juggling the date that
certain bills are paid. For instance, when medical
bills are received in late December, they should be
paid in either December or January, depending on
which would be most advantageous. Medical ex-

penses are deductible only when they exceed 3 percent of adjusted gross income. So if paying a medical bill in December still leaves you below the 3 percent level, you should defer payments until after January 1, since the deductions may help you on the following year's return.

EXEMPTIONS

The Most Efficient "Double" Exemptions

In addition to the exemptions to which you are entitled, you can actually claim a "double" exemption under certain circumstances. For instance, you are entitled to an extra $1,000 exemption beginning in the tax year in which you reach age 65. If you are "legally blind"—that is, your field of view does not exceed 20 degrees, or you cannot see better than 20/200 in the better eye with glasses—then you can claim an additional exemption, too.

The Most Efficient Way to Claim a Parent as an Exemption

For you to legally claim a parent as a dependent, he or she must (a) not have personal gross income exceeding $1,000 from sources other than you, and (b) more than half of his or her support must come from you. The $1,000 figure, however, does not include Social Security payments, and proceeds from life insurance, inheritances, or gifts.

The Fastest Way to Avoid Parental Regulations

True, legally to claim your parents as dependents, you must contribute more than half of their support. But if you technically don't contribute over 50 percent of the combined expenses of both parents, you still might be able to claim *one* of them as an exemption. For example, let's presume that you give your parents $2,500 a year, and together they need $7,000 to live on—or $3,500 each. If you tech-

nically give money to both of them, you're not entitled to any exemption, because the $2,500 is less
than half of their $7,000 living expenses. But if
you designate the $2,500 for only your mother,
that amount is over half of the $3,500 she alone
requires for her living costs. Thus, she can be
claimed as an exemption. Cancelled checks written
to your mother will prove to the IRS that she was
the recipient of the money.

The Efficient Way to Share Parental Exemptions

If several siblings share in the support of their
parents, probably none of them contributes more
than half of the support funds. But still, one of
them can take the exemption each year. Let's assume that four brothers each provide 25 percent of
their mother's living expenses. Each year, one (and
only one) of them can claim Mom as an exemption.
To be fair, they may want to alternate each year,
with each brother taking advantage of the exemption once every four years.

The Fastest Way of Beating the High Singles Tax Rate

Single people are penalized for their nonmarital
status by a higher tax rate. But you can beat this
elevated tax bite by qualifying as a "Head of Household." Singles, divorcees, and widows meet the cri-
teria for this special category if they are:

1. Unmarried on December 31.
2. Maintaining a household in which they pay over
   half the cost of its upkeep.
3. Allowing a dependent relative to use their house
   as his or her primary place of residence.

When you as a single person claim your mother
and/or father as a dependent(s), they need not be

living in your home for you to claim the Head of Household status. They can be residing, for instance, in a retirement or nursing home.

The Fastest Tax Credit Available

You can receive a tax credit of up to $500 if your earned income or adjusted gross income is less than $10,000, and if at least one dependent child lives with you. This is a "refundable" credit, and thus you are entitled to it even if you have no tax liability. An IRS office can provide details on the procedure for claiming your refund.

The Most Efficient Early Withdrawal of Time Deposits

Most banks and savings and loans offer a higher rate of interest to customers willing to deposit their money for a specified period of time—ranging from ninety days to ten years. But if you withdraw the money before the term expires, you must pay a penalty, usually an amount equal to the interest for a stipulated time. If you are required to forfeit some interest under these circumstances, the amount of the forfeiture can be deducted from your income taxes as a "loss incurred in a transaction entered upon for profit."

The Most Efficient Use of a Security Deposit

Landlords frequently demand a security deposit from their tenants that is equivalent to the last month's rent. State law often requires that these deposits be placed in a separate account and that interest be paid on them. The landlord, however, is usually allowed to take as an administrative expense an amount equal to 1 percent per year of this deposit. Under such circumstances, the tenant can deduct this 1 percent charge as an expense incurred for the "production of income."

The Fastest Means of Deducting Some Medical Costs

Medical expenses can often be deductible as business expenses, which is advantageous to the taxpayer. After all, medical expenses are deductible only when, in aggregate, they exceed 3 percent of an individual's adjusted gross income. Business expenses, however, are fully deductible.

When does a medical expense qualify as a business expense? According to the IRS, a medical cost may be deducted as a business cost if it is intrinsically related to a business activity. For example, consider a businessman confined to a wheelchair who takes his wife, an associate, or a nurse with him to an out-of-town business meeting to help him negotiate stairs and doors. The salary and expenses of this helper are deductible as a business expense, since they are essential in order for the businessman to conduct his affairs. Note that health insurance proceeds must be offset against itemized medical deductions.

The Most Efficient Health-Related Income Tax Saving

Some health-related income does not need to be counted when figuring out your taxes. Specifically, if you receive money from a health insurance policy (for which you paid the premiums), it is not taxable.

BUSINESS EXPENSES

The Most Efficient Way to Look for a Job

While you're pounding the pavement, keep track of the expenses you incur in the job-hunting process. You can deduct the costs of all job-seeking, including travel, meals, lodging, and agency fees.

However, if you are looking for your very first job, or a job in a new field, you *can't* deduct the costs.

The Most Efficient Business Deductions

If you incur expenses that are job-related and necessary for employment, you can deduct them on your income tax return. Here are some recent deductions that the IRS recently verified as legitimate:

- Business convention expenses.
- Costs of small tools.
- Uniforms used by pilots, bus drivers, doctors, nurses, firemen, mailmen, policemen, and porters.
- Union charges for out-of-work benefits.
- Trade association or Chamber of Commerce dues necessary for employment.
- Christmas gifts to employers, if such gift-giving is a standard practice.

The Cheapest Way to Move

You can significantly reduce the cost of moving if the move is job-related. Generally, if you changed job locations or started a new job, you may be able to deduct your moving expenses. The major stipulation for tax purposes is that your new job must be at least thirty-five miles farther from your former home than your old job location was. So if your old job was ten miles from home, your new job must be at least forty-five miles from that home.

The Fastest Way to Save on Gas

True, daily commuting expenses between home and work are not deductible, no matter what the distance or how high the cost of gas. But in this era when many people have two jobs, you *can* deduct the cost of getting from job #1 to job #2. If that commuting is done by car, you can deduct 18½ ¢ a mile for the first 15,000 miles a year, and 10¢ a mile thereafter.

The Cheapest Way to Get to Work

In the midst of the ongoing energy crisis, car pools are certainly advantageous for many reasons. By organizing one, you can't directly deduct the costs of your car repairs and gasoline. However, you do *not* have to include as income the reimbursement you receive from passengers for your auto expenses. So if you're charging your riders for the costs you incur, you won't have to pay taxes on it.

The Most Efficient Use of a Company Car

According to the IRS, if an individual uses a company car for his private use, that car must be considered as personal income. To avoid problems, keep a detailed log of when the car is used for business purposes and when it is used for personal transportation.

The Most Efficient Way to Buy Cigars

It is usually difficult to convince the IRS that the cost of cigars is tax-deductible. But if you are a businessman, the full cost of the cigars *is* deductible if you can show that you are a nonsmoker and are giving the cigars to clients.

The Fastest Way to Capitalize on the Cost of Watch Repairs

If a personal watch is required as part of your job, you may deduct the cost of repairs to it. For example, many employees of transportation companies, like railroads or airlines, are permitted to take this deduction.

The Most Efficient Use of a Hobby

Stamp or coin collecting, if done purely as a hobby, offers no tax benefits. But by attempting to make a profit from a hobby—for instance, by dealing in stamps or coins—you can legally deduct all your expenses or losses. If you are able to produce a profit in only two out of every five years, the IRS will presume that you are operating a legitimate business.

The Most Efficient Use of Military Uniforms

As a general rule, the purchase price and cleaning costs of a military uniform are not tax-deductible. However, an Armed Forces *reservist* can deduct the unreimbursed costs of his uniform if he is restricted from wearing it except while on duty as a reservist.

DEDUCTIBLE TAXES

Tax-Free Taxes

State income taxes are fully deductible from your federal income tax. Federal income taxes are not.

The Fastest Way to Capitalize on Disability Insurance

Many states have disability insurance laws which require that 1 percent of all employee wages be deposited in a state disability fund. All individuals subjected to this withholding are eligible for a federal tax deduction equal to that amount, since this payment is technically considered a state income tax.

The Fastest Way to Increase Sales-Tax Deductions

Money paid as state sales tax is deductible on your federal tax forms. An individual can concentrate these deductions in a particular year by making major purchases in a single twelve-month period. For instance, sales tax is paid on items like automobiles, boats, trailer homes, and construction materials. A 6 percent sales tax on a $7,000 car amounts to a $420 deduction. So make as many of these large purchases as possible in the year when large deductions may be particularly beneficial.

HOMEOWNER'S DEDUCTIONS

The Most Efficient Real Estate Deduction

The IRS won't argue about this one: if you own a home or a condominum that you rent, all expenses you have in renting and operating the property are deductible.

The Most Efficient Energy *and* Tax Savings

You are eligible for an energy tax credit if you insulate your home or install a heat pump and/or solar heater. This credit can save you up to $2,000 on your taxes, as well as decrease your home heating costs.

The Most Efficient Tax-Free Home Sale

Under special laws, you are permitted to sell your home and delay the capital gains tax if your home is replaced within certain time constraints: if within eighteen months before or eighteen months after the sale of your old home you buy and live in another home whose cost is at least as much as the sales price of the old home, the tax can be postponed.

The Most Efficient Way of Easing House-Sale Losses

Even in this era of soaring housing prices, some homeowners lose money in the sale of their houses. For instance, a new freeway nearby can lower the value of a home so dramatically that the owner will lose money in the transaction. Unfortunately, losses experienced in house sales are *not* tax-deductible. But nevertheless, there is a way to circumvent this IRS ruling. Try renting the house for a year or two before selling it; in that case, you can then legitimately deduct the "business loss," since the home has become "rental property."

The Most Efficient Use of a Vacation Home

If you own a house, apartment, or condominium that you sometimes rent out as a vacation home, you must be cautious about how you use it for your own personal pleasure. You cannot consider it a rental unit if you use the dwelling yourself for (a) more than fourteen days a year, or (b) more than 10 percent of the rental time—whichever is greater. So if you're interested in taking business deductions like maintenance, depreciation, and utilities, you must limit your own use of the premises.

The Most Efficient Prevention of Tax Sales

When you're very delinquent in paying your property taxes, your house may face a public tax sale, in which case it is sold to the highest bidder. However, you can avert this sale by paying the past due amount at any time until the sale is held. Even after the sale has occurred, you can often recover your house by paying the overdue taxes, as well as the penalty fee and the cost of holding the auction.

The Cheapest Real Estate Taxes

If you pay property taxes on time, you will avoid late payment penalties. Also, in many states a small discount on taxes is available if you pay your taxes in advance rather than adhering to a normal installment schedule.

The Fastest Way to Appeal Property Taxes

Real estate tax assessments can sometimes be reduced in the following way. First, find your property on the assessment rolls at the city or county assessor's office. Measure this assessment against that of comparable properties (similar type and size of house, lot size, etc.) in the same community. If your assessment is higher, you can complete a form in the assessor's office that will be a formal application for a reduction. Check with the assessor to determine the deadline for submitting appeals. If your request for a reduction is rejected, you can take the case to court.

DEDUCTIBLE INTEREST

Tax-Free Interest

In order to figure accurately the true cost of a loan to you, it's important to remember that interest is tax deductible. When deciding whether to take out a major loan, you would do well to subtract from the cost of the loan the tax saving you may make by being able to deduct your interest payments.

CHARITY

The Most Efficient Foster Care

Foster parents should take advantage of all the tax benefits available to them. Surprisingly, the most overlooked deduction is that foster parents may claim (as a charitable contribution) all their unreimbursed expenses for providing care for the children placed with them.

CASUALTY AND THEFT

The Most Efficient Way to Corroborate a Theft Loss

Theft losses in excess of $100 are deductible, but you must prove to the IRS that the loss wasn't caused by your own carelessness. Usually, by showing that you reacted responsibly after the theft—for instance, reporting the burglary promptly to the police—the IRS (and the insurance company) will be convinced.

The Fastest Way to Minimize a Disaster

When fire, flood, burglary, earthquake, or hurricane strikes, the tragedy can be minimized on your income tax forms. Uninsured casualty and theft losses in excess of $100 are deductible. So if an earthquake causes $1,000 uninsured damage to a home, $900 of that is deductible.

LEGAL FEES

The Most Efficient Divorce-Related Tax Advantage

Legal expenses for a divorce are not tax-deductible. However, as part of your attorney's services, you will probably be offered guidance on the tax ramifications of the dissolution. Ask the lawyer to give you an itemized bill, specifying the portion of the fee designated for this tax advice. That part of the bill is tax-deductible.

CHILD CARE

The Fastest Way to Reduce Child-Care Expenses

When you pay someone to care for a child under the age of fifteen, you may be able to take a tax credit of 20 percent of the child-care expenses. To take advantage of this tax savings, these child-related costs must be incurred in order to permit the parent to work.

The Most Efficient Tax-Deductible Granny

Though tax laws allow a deduction of up to $400

a month for child care in order to allow a parent to work, the deduction isn't permitted for payments to a relative closer than a cousin. Some families believe this erodes the grandmother's traditional job, and many are exchanging each other's grannies' day-care services to get the deduction. The tax-avoidance ploy is called "The Granny Switch."

BOARDERS

The Cheapest Boarder in Your House

If a full-time student—other than one of your dependents—lives in your home, you can deduct your expenses in supporting him, as long as your boarder is in the twelfth or any lower grade. The student may be either a foreign or an American student.

ONCE YOU'VE FILED

The Fastest Way to Obtain a Tax Filing Extension

A taxpayer who is unable to submit his income tax return by April 15 can quickly—and automatically—obtain a two-month extension of the filing deadline by completing and submitting IRS Form 4868 before April 15. On that form, an estimate must be given of what the tax will be. If that estimate exceeds what has already been paid through withholding, a check for the balance must accompany the form. No late penalty is required under this procedure, but if an individual *underestimates* by more than 10 percent, an interest charge will eventually be levied on the amount still due, plus a penalty of one half of 1 percent a month until the difference is paid.

The Most Efficient Way to Capitalize on Late Payments

When you are charged interest by the IRS for paying your taxes late, you can soften the blow by deducting these interest payments on your return for the year the interest was paid.

The Fastest Way to Earn Government Interest

The inefficiencies of the federal bureaucracy sometimes have payoffs for taxpayers. For instance, if you are owed a refund on the tax return you file, the government must begin paying you interest on it if the refund is not made within forty-five days of the return's due date. So if you file the return on April 15, and the refund arrives after May 31, you will earn interest on the money, beginning on June 1.

The Most Efficient Time to Save Tax Records

According to the IRS, you should keep your income tax records for a minimum of three full years after the April 15 filing date. Actually, if an audit is going to be conducted, it will almost always be done within twenty-six months of its filing. But to be safe, the three-year time span is suggested. So the tax records for the return you filed on April 15, 1981, should be kept at least until April 15, 1984.

The Fastest Way to Obtain Old Tax Returns

Have you lost or destroyed copies of your old tax returns? Copies of them dating back as far as six years can be obtained directly from the IRS. Simply fill out Form 4506 ("Request for Copy of Tax Return") and mail it to the address on the form.

The Fastest Way to Trigger an IRS Audit

Only about one of forty individuals will be subjected to an audit of their tax return in any single year. The trouble spots that are most likely to provoke an audit include:

— Suspicion of unreported income: do your deductions seem curiously high in relation to your reported income?
— Large purchases of tax-exempt bonds: the interest on money borrowed to buy municipal securities is not deductible.
— Combined business-pleasure trips: the IRS will want a complete accounting of the trips, including the time and money spent on business.
— Home office deduction: under current rulings, you can deduct part of the operating and depreciation expenses of your home only if a room in it is used regularly and *exclusively* for business purposes.

The Most Efficient Way of Avoiding an Audit

When a valid but unusual deduction is claimed, an audit can often be prevented by attaching photocopies of the appropriate supporting documents or receipts. Don't send originals—keep them in your files and submit copies only.

The Most Effective Tax Audit Advice

The date on which you file your income tax return has no effect on whether yours is flagged by the computer for audit. Some people file early, according to the IRS, because they believe that the government expects cheaters to wait until the last minute. Others wait until the deadline to send in their returns and hope theirs will be overlooked in the deluge. The truth is that all returns are checked by computer for completeness, errors in arithmetic, and nonallowable deductions. In fact, there is only one way timing may trigger an audit. If you wait until the last minute, you are more apt to make just those errors the computer has been programmed to catch.

The Most Efficient Handling of an Audit

Most audits are routine, and there's little reason to be nervous if you can verify your income and/or deductions. For the audit to be as much in your favor as possible, request an office rather than a field audit. An office audit is more advantageous to you, usually requiring that you bring cancelled checks and signed receipts to the nearest IRS office. A field audit, however, is conducted at your place of business or home, and necessitates that you make available much more information, including record books and files.

The Most Efficient Way to Appeal an Auditor's Findings

After an audit, it is not uncommon for a taxpayer to disagree with an auditor's findings. If that happens to you, *don't* sign a waiver agreement (Form 870) verifying that you concur with this ruling. Instead, appeal the decision, first with the auditor's immediate supervisor, whom you can meet with immediately. If you're still dissatisfied after that session, make an appointment with the "appellate conferee." You can also take your complaint directly to the Tax Court, which is independent of the IRS.

Cheapest Tax Challenge

Ten dollars is all it will cost you to take the IRS to court if you are wrangling with it over how much tax you owe and the disputed amount is $1500 or less. The court is Small Claims Tax Court and it operates under the same principles as the Small Claims part of Civil Court: it's cheap, fast, and you don't need a lawyer (although you can hire one). You tell your side of the dispute to the judge in your own words and if he finds for you the IRS has to leave you alone—at least for this year. However, the judge's decision is final; if he rules against you, you can't then appeal.

To get a case into Small Claims Tax Court, the IRS has to start the fight by sending you an official Notice of Deficiency. You then have ninety days to file your petition for a hearing by writing to the U.S. Tax Court in Washington, D.C. Cases are heard all around the country and the government notifies you when and where yours is scheduled. Although there are no official records of who is ahead, your chances of winning are good. Even the government admits—off the record—that there are more winning defendants than losing ones.

Chapter 12
TRAVEL AND TOURISM

TRAVEL BASICS
BEFORE YOU GO

Best Way to Learn About Your Destination

Go to the library. Take out books on the country or countries you intend to visit. And check the index of back issues of magazines such as *Travel & Leisure, Holiday* and *Gourmet* (it carries wonderful travel articles). The better informed you are about a place, the more you'll enjoy it.

Anticipate Emergency Calls

Not just your final travel destination but your entire itinerary should be made available to a neighbor or relative prior to departure, just in case someone needs to get in touch. If you're traveling by car, include its description and license number so local police can find you if necessary.

Packing Soft-Sided Luggage

Your possessions can easily be damaged in soft-sided luggage. Buy toiletries in plastic tubes and containers when possible and pack jars and bottles carefully. Remember that even jewelry, if not thoroughly wrapped, can be dented if the luggage is dropped or has a heavy object placed on it.

Best Way to Protect Your Jewelry

Leave it at home. Substitute costume jewelry for your valuables and you'll eliminate worry as well as possible loss.

Handiest Tool

A pocketknife—good for picnics, slicing the local fruit, cutting a loose thread, or any other small task that may come up.

Best Way to Prepare for Rainy Weather

Pack a folding umbrella and a thin plastic raincoat that can be wiped thoroughly dry and packed away. Bulky raincoats are hard to pack and a nuisance when wet.

Pack Your Own Paper

Take along your own writing paper and note cards—it's often hard to find a shop open at the right place and the right hour.

Pack Sewing, First-Aid Kits and Medicines

On an extended trip pack a small sewing kit, first-aid kit, and all regularly used cosmetics and toiletries. Don't waste precious time hunting for them in shops when you're in an unfamiliar city or a strange country. Also bring along an ample supply of your own prescription drugs. These can't be replaced abroad.

Plan Ahead for Shopping

Pack an empty, sturdy, capacious canvas bag for souvenirs, gifts, and general shopping expeditions.

The Traveling Photographer

When traveling with a camera, take along pre-addressed envelopes suitable for mailing your exposed film to the developer you use—your pictures will be waiting for you when you get home.

Cheapest Way to Pack for Auto Travel

Pack light. It is tempting to load your car with everything you might possibly need on your vacation but that convenience may be costly. The lighter the car, the less gas it uses. The U.S. Department of Energy estimates that each hundred pounds decreases fuel economy about 1 percent for the average car and 1¼ percent for small cars.

How to Find the Cheapest Fare Between Two Points

Call every airline which services your destination, or insist that your travel agent make a similar check. Airlines seldom have the same (and sometimes not even similar) fares between the same two cities under present regulations.

Cheapest airfares usually involve off-hours and mid-weekday travel, with prepaid advance ticket purchases.

Pay Now, Fly Later

Increased fuel costs mean increased and increasing flight costs. Pay for your tickets as far in advance as possible; you will not be affected by any later price hike.

How to Insure That Policy

Although it is mostly sold at airports, travelers' insurance covers every form of transportation and could be an inexpensive way of lessening your worries. For anyone who travels regularly, even to and from work, it might be worth considering.

Be sure to take a stamped, preaddressed envelope with you to the airport if you plan to buy insurance before a flight and mail the policy home, or to whomever you choose—it doesn't make sense to have it on the plane with you, just in case!

Most Efficient Way to Avoid Religious Freaks (and the like) at the Airport

Most airlines have "clubs" of various kinds which provide comfortable, well-equipped waiting rooms, closed to the general public, at major airports. Anyone can join for under $50 per year. These were open by invitation only until a lawsuit a few years ago opened them to everyone who could pay. Details are usually available in timetables or by writing to the airlines.

Best Way to Prepare for a Long Flight

Get your entire body in condition. Running, fast walking, jogging, cycling, or swimming two or three times a week and for at least two weeks before departure will help you to feel fit while traveling.

Cheapest Cocktails on Flights

Your own thermos of bloody marys or whiskey sours will not only save you money on the plane but will probably taste better than the airlines. Just ask the hostess for ice and glasses.

How to Stay Entertained on Board

If you're flying with a companion, about four

games of Scrabble (or try the new game, Boggle) will take you from one side of the country to the other. it's even easier to pack a deck of cards for "21" or gin rummy; many airlines give them out free.

Best Flight Insurance for Foot Comfort

Pack a pair of soft slippers in your carry-on luggage.

Easiest Way to Stay Fresh While Flying

On long trips, the point is to keep your muscles in tone, key joints flexible, and your circulation going. The answer is exercise. Try jogging in place by raising your heels alternately. At the same time, raise your arms in a bent position and rock rhythmically forward and back as if you were walking.

To improve circulation in your legs, sit with elbows on your knees, bending forward with your weight pressed downward. Lift up on your toes as high as possible and drop your heels. Repeat thirty times.

To relax shoulder muscles, move your shoulders gently and rhythmically in large circles, forward and backward.

Exercise your ankle joints by rolling your feet in large circles. Repeat fifteen times in each direction.

And stand up, get a drink of water, and walk around!

Fastest Airport Checkout

Tired of waiting around airports for your luggage to show up on that conveyor belt? Try taking your luggage with you. Some of the new suitcases allow you to pack an entire wardrobe into a bag that will fit under the airplane seat. Overseas travelers can bring on board luggage whose combined length, width, and height doesn't exceed 45 inches. And not only do you save time, you also avoid having

your luggage arrive at a different airport than you
do.

Most Efficient Way to Make Telephone Calls from Airports and Railroad Stations

Instead of fumbling with dimes and quarters to
tell the people at home that you've arrived safely
(or late), use the coinless pay phones designed for
collect or credit card calls (fewer people use these)
or else simply use one dime, which is returned, to
make a credit card or collect call from an ordinary
pay phone. In some cities, assisted long-distance
service is provided: you tell the attendant which
number you are calling and then pick up the re-
ceiver in an assigned telephone booth, paying after
the call is completed.

Cheapest Airline Complaint Hot-Line

If you have bumping, baggage, or other flight
complaints, put in a call to the Office of the Consumer Advocate at the Civil Aeronautics Board, 1825
Connecticut Avenue NW, Washington, D.C. 20428—
202-382-7735. Though you will pay for the first
three minutes, they will call you back if more time
is required.

CHEAP LODGING

Cheapest Sleeping Quarters

Travel during the night by train, bus, or boat
and you will be saving the cost of a hotel room as
well as making the most efficient use of your vacation hours.

How to Be at Home Wherever You Go

Even with the increasing cost of fuel, a rented
trailer can still be a pretty good way to enjoy a
family holiday, especially if the family car is up to

the strain of towing. There are trailer camps in many countries, some better than others, and the savings in hotel and motel bills and restaurant meals can make the effort worthwhile.

Cheapest Vacation Home

Is a trade. Exchange your house or apartment with someone in the area you wish to visit. You may even find that a car becomes part of the deal. There are a number of services that offer these listings. The Vacation Exchange Club, 350 Broadway, New York, New York 10013, offers a subscription to two publications plus one listing for $15. For about the same price you can receive three directories and one listing from the International Home Exchange Service, Box 3975, San Francisco, California 94119 or a subscription and listing with the Interservice Home Exchange, Box 87, Glen Echo, Maryland 20768.

UNPACKING

Cheapest Tailor

If your clothes need pressing when you unpack, hang them neatly in the bathroom (on plastic or wooden clothes hangers) and then fill the tub with very hot water. Keep the door closed to allow the steam time to work its way into those wrinkles and smooth them out. If your room has a shower instead of a tub, economize on energy by letting your clothes get part of their steam during the time you are taking your shower.

Easiest Way to Minimize Wrinkling

Unpack when you arrive. Hang up clothing as soon as possible so that wrinkles will fall out. If your clothes are packed with tissue paper in the folds of the garments, it helps to reduce wrinkling from the start.

KIDS

Lost Any Kids Lately?

Most children don't know where they are, especially when traveling, but that doesn't stop them from wandering away on occasion. Tag them: name, local address (hotel or wherever), and phone number.

Similar tagging could be helpful when you take kids shopping or sightseeing in the city. You can't hold hands all the time, and in a crowded scene they may be too small to find.

SEE THE U.S.A.

Fastest Travel Information

For a complete rundown on places, facilities, and just about anything else that might interest a vacationer, dial the USA Travel Information Center's toll-free number 800-323-4180 (in Illinois, dial 800-942-4833).

GETTING THERE

Cheapest Long-Distance Travel

For those who travel a lot, People Transient of Oregon offers a unique way of cutting down on expenses while helping to save the country's energy. They run a nationwide, long-distance car and airplane pool. For a $125 lifetime membership fee, they will match up potential riders with potential drivers and pilots wanting to take a trip of 300 miles or more. The travelers split the costs, thereby saving a substantial amount of money.

For those wishing to take advantage of their service on a short-term basis, one-year memberships are available for $40, and six-month memberships for $25. As to what your chances are of being matched up for the trip you'd like to take, the company claims that with five days' notice they have a 90 percent success rate. Their phone number is 800-547-0933.

Cheapest Way to Obtain Road and other Maps

Exxon is one of the very few oil companies that still provides free road maps and street plans of cities, available at gas stations and touring centers in major cities. Otherwise, try writing to city Chambers of Commerce or state or foreign tourist agencies, or Xeroxing maps in public libraries.

How to Obtain Free Baggage Service

Many Amtrak trains provide free baggage service up to 150 pounds. If you have a ticket, checked baggage will be accepted up to thirty minutes before departure and will be available for pick-up within thirty minutes after arrival. Since not all trains offer this service, you may want to plan your travel time accordingly.

How to Get Special Services

Amtrak provides special assistance for handicapped, elderly, and any other passenger who needs help in stations or on board trains. Telephone ahead for assistance with baggage, for a wheelchair, or for help in boarding the train. Call the toll-free reservation number.

Essentially the same services are offered by airlines; again, call the toll-free number to make arrangements.

Most Efficient Way to Travel Between New York and Washington (or Boston)

The Eastern Air Shuttle leaves hourly from La Guardia. No reservations are necessary (or accepted), fares ($48 one-way to Boston, $51 to Washing-

ton) are collected on board, and flight time can be
as little as forty-three minutes. If the number of
passengers exceeds seats available, the airline simply provides an additional plane. There are reduced
fares on weekends.

Cheapest Weekend Vacation

Try your own hometown. Many motels and hotels, some with elaborate resort facilities, offer special weekend packages in their off-seasons for
couples or families. One or more may be in your
hometown. A carefree weekend in a hometown hotel
or resort can be just as relaxing and enjoyable as
one spent hundreds of miles away—even more so,
when you consider the transportation costs you'll
be saving, not to mention the extra time you'll have
since you won't have to travel. Other people probably come hundreds of miles to spend a weekend at
some terrific vacation spot within ten miles of where
you live. You can have the same fun at much less
expense. One tip, though—don't tell your friends
where you're going.

Most Efficient Way to Make Hotel Reservations

In the U.S., hotel chains have their own toll-free
numbers to call. In Europe, almost every train station and airport has a welcome service that will
reserve a hotel room for you on the spot before
putting you into a taxi or bus to the city. The
Netherlands, for example, has a nation-wide number for reservations anywhere in Holland free of
charge.

. . . Especially by Not Driving into Town

Plan your trip so that you stop for the night
before you come anywhere near a big city, as much
as twenty-five to fifty miles before. It will keep you
out of the late afternoon and early evening traffic
in and around the city itself when you are already
tired from the day's driving. Also, it probably puts

you in a motel area which, because it is not too close to the city, is less expensive and more likely to have vacancies.

Next day, after breakfast, you'll be able to tackle the city's traffic with renewed alertness.

U.S. TRAVEL TIPS

Cheapest Rapid Transit Fares for the General Public

In most cities, including New York, Philadelphia, and Los Angeles, there are various reduced fare plans, including "Shoppers' Buses" (either special buses or special fares on the regular buses), covering the central downtown shopping areas. Los Angeles and other cities allow unlimited travel over certain periods at reduced fares, and New York has reduced fares on weekends and low-fare night travel at certain times. Information is usually available from Chambers of Commerce or special local telephone numbers.

Cheapest Way to Get Around in Philadelphia

Those over 65 can enjoy unlimited free travel on the city's transit lines, except during rush hours, after having obtained senior citizen passes. The program was established by former governor Milton Shapp. In other cities senior citizens generally pay half fare.

Most Efficient U.S. Restaurant Guide

Mobil (the oil company) puts out an annual *City Vacation and Business Guide* which gives information on hotels, motels restaurants and sightseeing in fifty-eight U.S. cities and contains discount certificates for certain attractions. The book costs $4.95 (published by Rand McNally) but is available for less at discount book stores in some large cities. If you read French, the *Guide Bleu*, published by

Hachette, is about as good but much more expensive (it is available at large libraries).

U.S. SIGHTS

Cheapest Boat-Bus Tour in the Northeast

The National Park Service has a free, three-hour tour of the old mill town of Lowell, Massachusetts, which includes a trip through its canal and gatehouse system. For information or reservations write to the Lowell National Historical Park, at 171 Merrimack Street, Lowell, Massachusetts 01851 or phone 617-459-4136.

Investigate National Park Service offerings wherever you go. They are becoming increasingly varied and imaginative. Near Fredericksburg, Virginia, you can watch an eighteenth century farm at work. At Hopewell Village in Elverson, Pennsylvania, a nineteenth century iron-making village comes alive before your eyes. There are presentations in national parks and forests across the country—and they are all free.

Cheapest Entree to National Parks

A Golden Eagle Passport will admit the bearer and a carload of passengers to national parks and recreation areas throughout the country for the year in which it was purchased. There is no limit to the number of times it may be used. The Passport costs $12 and may be purchased at regional park or forest service offices or by writing to the National Park Service Headquarters, U.S. Department of Interior, Washington, D.C. 20240, or to the Forest Service Headquarters, U.S. Department of Agriculture, Washington, D.C. 20250.

For those who are sixty-two or older, there is a free lifetime Golden Age Passport which can be obtained at any regional office of the National Park System or Forest Service by showing proof of age.

Cheapest Way to Tour Our National Parks

The U.S. Department of the Interior offers a Golden Eagle Passport which admits the holder and everyone accompanying him or her in a private, noncommercial vehicle free entrance to all the national parks, monuments, historic sites, and recreation areas administered by the National Park Service for one calendar year. The Golden Eagle Passport costs $12, and for families who do a lot of traveling together it can be an excellent buy. For those sixty-two and older, a Golden Age Passport, which provides the same advantages on a lifetime basis, is available free. This one also provides a 50 percent discount on federal use fees in the areas involved.

The Passports are available at many of the parks themselves, but to be on the safe side write before your trip to the National Park Service, Room 1013, U.S. Department of the Interior, 18th and C Streets NW, Washington, D.C. 20240.

TRAVELING ABROAD
BEFORE YOU GO

Cheapest Way to Research Your Destination

The more you know about the country you visit, the more likely you are to enjoy it. For 70¢ you can become an expert on any country's people, history, politics, and economy. Just send the money to the Superintendent of Documents, U.S. Government Printing Office, Washington, D.C. 20402, and ask for a pamphlet on the country you want in their "Background Notes on the Countries of the World" series.

Rock Bottom Vacations

If you would like your vacation to be both different and inexpensive, Earthwatch might be your answer. Their expeditions have included ecological studies at Cape Cod and archeological investigations in Peru—manned mostly by inexperienced amateurs under the guidance of experts. Earthwatch is a nonprofit organization whose low costs (designated "contributions") are tax-deductible.

For more information write to them at 10 Juniper Road, Box 127, Belmont, Massachusetts 02178.

Best Way to See Ireland

A visit to Ireland is probably one of the most worthwhile things you could ever do, and one of the best—and cheapest—ways to do it is through a program sponsored by the Council on International Educational Exchange and the Irish Union of Students. The "Encounter Ireland Program," a four-week educational and travel experience, gives you a privileged look at Ireland's history and culture for only about $800 to $900. Included is your transportation to and from Ireland, room and board with a family in Dublin for three weeks, and various other benefits. Write the CIEE at 777 United Nations Plaza, New York, New York 10017 for more details.

Best Source of Benefits for Students Traveling Abroad

The Special International Student Identity Card can open your way to a wide variety of discounts on foreign travel, lodging, and the like in many countries around the world. The card is available at a low cost from the Council of International Educational Exchange, 777 United Nations Plaza, New York, New York, 10017. The CIEE is also a great source of free or inexpensive publications which can be of great use to any student planning to travel abroad.

Cheapest Shopping

Most people are aware that the duty-free allowance on purchases made out of the country is now $300. But how many know that for countries classified as "most favored nations," like Malaysia, Israel, Angola, and Chile, much of what they grow, manufacture, or produce is exempt from import duties?

For a full list of these nations, request the free booklet, "GSP and the Traveler," from your nearest Customs representative or write to the U.S. Customs Service, 1301 Constitution Avenue NW, Washington, D.C. 20229. For other customs rules, the booklet to ask for is "Know Before You Go."

How to Learn Items Permitted or Prohibited

Going out of the country? For a list of items permitted and prohibited—foods, plants, and plant or animal products—write to: "Travelers Tips," U.S. Department of Agriculture, Washington, D.C. 20250.

Fastest Way to Find a Foreign Doctor

You can obtain a free list of English-speaking foreign doctors from the International Association for Medical Assistance to Travelers, 350 Fifth Avenue, New York, New York 10001. Physicians in 500 cities in 116 countries are included on the list, all of whom have agreed to charge no more than $15 for an office visit and $20 for a hotel or house call.

GETTING THERE

The Cheapest Flight to Europe

Icelandic, which never joined the fare-regulating agency International Air Transport Association

(IATA), charges less than the fixed IATA fares. Depending on the time of year and the time of day, flights cost from 15 to 44 percent less than the IATA-approved flights. En route to Europe, all Icelandic flights stop in Reykjavik, the capital of Iceland, and then proceed only to Luxembourg on the European continent. You are allowed two free pieces of baggage, the sum of whose dimensions must not exceed 107 inches.

Laker Airways is the most inexpensive direct flight to London. You buy your ticket for travel the same day or, if all flights are full, for the next available flight.

Cheapest Way to Fly to London

Due to the rising fuel costs, flying is getting expensive again after a relatively short period of low costs following the deregulation of the airline industry. Bargains are still to be found, however, particularly if you're interested in going from New York to London. A one-way New York–London ticket cost only $135 recently, while a round-trip ticket was $254. (Prices will probably have risen slightly by the time this book reaches the bookstores.) There is one drawback to the Laker plan, however—there are no reservations for the cutrate fares. All tickets must be purchased on the day of departure at one of the Laker outlets in New York City and London. For more information, consult your travel agent or the Laker Travel Center, 95-25 Queens Boulevard, Rego Park, New York 11374, (212) 459-6092.

ONCE YOU'RE THERE

Best Way to Exchange Your Dollars

Trade your money for foreign currency at an airport exchange or at a bank rather than at your hotel—you'll get more for your money. Buy small amounts of foreign currency before you go, especially for the country you will visit first; banking facilities may be closed on the day and hour of your arrival.

Cheapest Place to Cash Travelers' Checks

At the bank. Many other places add sizable charges for the service.

Cheapest Coins

While bills can be converted across borders, coins you take out of a country are almost always worthless. Be sure to dispose of coins before you leave the country you're visiting.

Easiest Way to Keep Your Money Straight on Foreign Soil

Carry two change purses. As soon as you leave the country, pack away American money and keep foreign change handy. Reverse the procedure when you are preparing your return trip.

Cheapest Phone Calls

The cheapest calls are NOT the ones made from your hotel. Most hotels charge for the service—and some tack on really outrageous amounts. Make your calls from public booths, particularly those at the post office or telegraph center if you'll need coins or additional assistance.

Cheapest Quality Lodging in Europe

When traveling in Europe, the cheapest lodging is also the best. Spread across the continent are hundreds of youth hostels. The name is misleading: the hostels are not meant just for youth but for all economy-minded travelers.

One of the most interesting aspects of the hostels is the friendly common room. Settle down here to rest after a day's exploring and you find yourself drawn into easy and fascinating conversation with people of many different countries. Don't be afraid of a language barrier, because most Europeans speak two or more languages, and there will always be someone to translate for those who can't speak English. Most of these people are on extended trips and you're bound to meet some who have just been where you're heading and can give you the benefit of their experiences. The best and the friendliest hostels are in the countryside. Those in the major cities are sometimes overrun with screaming kids and burdened with curfews and restrictions.

Accommodations are a mixture of dormitories and private rooms, and a kitchen is usually provided for the guests' use. The kitchens are another place where friends are made, and with a bit of luck you could find yourself sharing in a feast of many lands. All this comes at a fraction of the cost of even moderately priced hotels. Note: hostels have their drawbacks; in some there are age limits, many hostels are outside the city, and transportation to the hostel at night can be a problem.

Best Cheap Hotel in Paris

Hotels are relatively inexpensive in Paris in comparison to those in other major European cities, but some are still better bargains than others. One of the best—for price, location, and congeniality—is the Hotel Cluny Square on the corner of the Boulevard St. Michel and the Boulevard St. Germain. A single without shower in the hotel, located right in the heart of the Latin Quarter, is only 40 francs ($10.00), breakfast included. The proprietors are also quite friendly. Caution: these hotels may have rooms which overlook noisy boulevards.

Cheapest Way to Get Around Paris

Unless you're loaded, you're undoubtedly going to be using the public transportation system extensively when you're in Paris. Rather than paying two francs every time you get on the bus or métro, consider buying a carnet—a book of 10 second-class tickets for only 12.5 francs. You save about 7.5 francs (approximately $2), and you can buy as many carnets as you like. They are available at any métro stop. And, if you're going to be in Paris for a month, inquire about the special monthly passes that could save you even more money.

Cheapest Restaurant Meal

Check the menu for a fixed-price meal. This can result in as much as 50 percent saving over a similar dinner ordered a la carte.

Cheapest Transportation in Towns

The cheapest transportation in each town is, of course, the public transportation—but it may be a lot cheaper than you expect! In Bologna, Italy, for instance, all public transportation is free from the beginning of service until nine in the morning and from 4:30 until 8:00 P.M. Other towns have special rates for ten trips or offer a weekly ticket. Check at the tourist office as soon as you arrive in town. And remember, in much of Europe the public transportation is clean and efficient, but sometimes—as with the Louvre station on the Paris métro—it is also a sightseeing "must."

Senior Citizen Super-Savers

Many countries offer substantial transportation reductions for older people. For example, in Austria a man over sixty-five or a woman over sixty can purchase I.D. cards at the railroad station that grant a 50 percent discount on trains and buses and even on some boat trips. The tourist office of the country you plan to visit or your travel agent can supply you with the information.

Cheapest Way to Travel from London to Edinburgh

Although the rail system in Britain is efficient and reasonably priced, you can still save a few pounds by traveling on the buses at night. For instance, it will cost you only about nine pounds to go from London to Edinburgh if you are willing to travel at night. Buses are available to Glasgow as well for the same price at the same hour. For more details, check at the information desk at the bus station in London.

Cheapest Way to Fly Around Europe

Although most students don't know about them, there are many special flights in Europe itself which offer low rates to undergraduates and graduate students. The flights are sponsored by the Student Air Travel Association. In order to be eligible, you must be a full-time student under 30 or the child or spouse of someone who fulfills the SATA requirements. See a travel agent in Europe for more details.

Cheapest Way to Get Around Europe

Traveling around Europe these days can be a rather expensive proposition if you're not fond of hitchhiking. The cost of renting a car and driving around the continent is astronomical, considering that gasoline in Europe is approximately three times as expensive as it is in the United States. Probably your best bet is to take the trains, and if you get one of the special rail passes available to Americans, you could save a bundle.

For instance, a Eurail pass, which must be purchased in the United States, gives you unlimited travel in fifteen countries on the continent plus reduced fares on buses and boats, for a very reasonable price. The 1980 charge was $190 for fifteen days, $230 for twenty-one days, $280 for one month, $380 for two months, and $460 for three months.

And, if you're under twenty-six, you are entitled to an even bigger bargain—the Eurail Youth Pass. This pass will give you two months of unlimited travel in fifteen countries for only about $260 (the 1980 charge). (Prices will undoubtedly increase 10—15 percent to keep up with inflation.) The countries participating in this plan include Austria, Belgium, Denmark, Finland, France, Greece, Holland, Italy, Luxembourg, Norway, Portugal, Spain, Sweden, Switzerland, and West Germany. (Guard your pass carefully, all passes are nonreplaceable and nonrefundable if lost or stolen.) Consult your travel agent for details.

And if you're interested in a similar pass for Britain, ask about the Britrail Pass, which entitles you to about fourteen days of unlimited train travel around England, Scotland, and Wales for around $100.

GIFTS FOR HOME

Cheapest Gifts

Foods from other countries rate high, but so many travelers have discovered this that some recipients are becoming innundated with saffron from Spain, pignola nuts from Italy, and jam from England. An innovative idea for a small cash outlay is a gift of foreign wrapping paper or note cards—and they have the added advantage of being light to carry.

Buy some greeting cards for your own future use. "Happy Birthday" or "Get Well" in another language somehow seems more special.

Cheapest Way to Buy Gifts and Souvenirs

Shop in the local equivalent of five-and-dime stores, in hardware stores, and inexpensive department stores. Search out craft articles indigenous to the country—paper flowers and baskets in Mexico, for example, plastic kitchenware in Italy, scarves in France. *Avoid expensive tourist traps!* Shop where the natives shop.

Chapter 13
RECREATION

AT HOME TV

Most Efficient TV Watching

Plan your watching. Sit down with a TV schedule each day or each week and decide what you want to watch. Then don't turn on the set until it's time for your program to come on the air. And most important, turn the set off as soon as what you've decided to watch is over. You'll be surprised how much time (not to mention energy) you'll save.

Efficient Way to Adjust Antenna

To aim an antenna, have a friend rotate it while you watch the picture on your set. Measure the exposure by your weakest station. When that picture looks good, your antenna is pointed in the right direction.

Most Efficient TV Reception Free of CB Interference

Hundreds of thousands of television viewers receive bursts of diagonal lines across their screens on channels 2, 5, or 9 because of proliferating citizens band radios. This annoyance can often be stopped with a simple "high pass" filter attached to the TV antenna. The filter can be bought for about $5 at electronics stores or obtained—often free—from the TV manufacturer or retailer.

Cheapest Way to Operate an "Instant-On" TV

Remember, that "instant-on" feature is using energy even when the screen is dark. There are a number of ways to eliminate this waste. The simplest is to unplug the set from the wall socket when it is not in use—but not all sockets are easily accessible. Buying an extension cord with an off-on switch may simplify the problem of reaching it. Plugging the set into an outlet that is controlled by a wall switch is another alternative. And finally, if you have any electrical know-how, you can install an off-on switch right on the power cord of the TV set.

PETS

Cheapest Pet

The common ant. Ant farms can be purchased in most toy stores for about $9, costing less then 1¢ per pet. Costs can be lowered by making the ant farm yourself. All you need is a sectioned box, dirt, some crumbs, a glass cover, and the readily available livestock. You will be rewarded by many enjoyable hours of watching these industrious little creatures at work. You won't be able to cuddle these

tiny pets, but on the plus side they don't need shots
and neutering is unnecessary.

Cheapest Way to Learn About Your Dog

The American Kennel Club, at 51 Madison Avenue, New York, New York 10010, is the national
authority on dog shows and most activities in the
world of dogs. It is a nonprofit corporation and
maintains an extensive library. A letter to the li-
brarian at the club offices will bring general information about reference works on your breed of
dog. Veterinary information, however, will not be
furnished.

Cheapest Way to Learn About Other Pets

Goldfish and other pets are described in 75¢ books
published by T.F.H. Publications, 11 Sylvania Avenue, Neptune, New Jersey 07553. These small but
useful books are usually found on pet department
shelves. A letter to the company will bring a copy
of the current list of books available if your pet
store doesn't carry them.

Cheapest Bird Feeder

Buy one of those discounted overage loaves of
packaged bread. Poke holes in the paper wrapper.
Insert a series of twigs or sticks through the width
of the bread, making sure they extend out far
enough to act as perches for the birds. Then hang
the bread outside your window or from the upper
branch of a tree. The birds will have no difficulty
discovering this treat.

Efficient Way to Test Bird Food on Your Birds

This is an experiment. Build a tray with at least
six compartments of equal size that birds can feed
from. Fill each compartment with a different kind
of food, and see how quickly each compartment is
emptied. While you can assume that the food that

disappears most rapidly is the most favored, your guests may have special tastes, and not even the most popular food will satisfy a bird with discriminating taste.

Cheapest Bird Food

Food that has been cast aside by stores because it was contained in a broken glass or is stale or over-ripe is a great bargain for your birds. Also, ask your butcher for fatty meat. Use your leftovers.

Buying a Good Guitar Cheap

The place used to be pawnshops, but pawnbrokers have become more shrewd as the demand for guitars has increased in the last ten years. The place to look for guitar bargains is in the classifieds. Many people find old guitars in their attics and, because the instruments are old and dusty, assume they have little worth. Look for Gibsons, Guilds, Martins, Epiphones, Vegas.

Also, some of the early Japanese guitars initially hit the market at around $100. Many were surprisingly good—some Yamahas, for example—and are sometimes resold cheaply because they were inexpensive new.

With electric guitars, certain "sounds" come and go, altering a guitar's market value regardless of the quality of its workmanship. For example, Fender *Jaquars* and *Jazzmasters* were top of the line instruments when they were made, but their "sound" (these were *the* guitars of the "surfing sound") is no longer desirable to most musicians. Both of these can usually be purchased secondhand for substantially less than their original list price, even in music stores and pawnshops.

But the classifieds are still the place to look. One friend bought a vintage *Les Paul* Gibson this way for $100; the seller was apologizing for its dustiness and its crummy case. Its value on the market is $600 to $1,000.

Stretching the Life of Guitar Strings

Old steel guitar strings can be brought back to life by boiling them in water. This removes the grit and oil which deadens the strings.

Cheapest Musical Instrument

Your own body. The art of hambone—playing rhythms on your chest, thighs, head, arms, etc.—turns the anatomy into a human trap set. Properly played, the various appendages and surfaces produce a surprising range of timbres and allow a rhythmic sophistication limited only by your own talent. Shoeshine boys can often help in your instruction.

OUTDOORS

Cheapest Good Running Shoe

A good running shoe can no longer be bought for under $20 at a retail store. But for $21 the Adidas *Dragon* is a good, durable, all-round shoe. Although not the best shoe on the market, it is an unmatched value for the price. For $24, the Saucony *Hornet* is a gem—a shoe comparable in its impact protection, flexibility, and comfort to many shoes twice the price. Other good shoes for less than $25 are the Adidas *Orion*, the Nike *Roadrunner I*, and the Brooks *Villanova*.

Fastest Way to Run in Sand

Step down as flat-footed as possible, placing neither the toe nor the heel first, both of which will sink your foot too deeply in the sand. Running flat-footed is a technique devised and first used by Australian lifeguards for running events in their annual tournaments.

How to Teach a Child to Swim

Swimming lessons for a child can begin at home in your own bathtub or in a wash basin. That's where your child can be taught to breathe properly, to keep eyes open under water—and to lose the fear of this strange new element. You can make a game of it.

Swimming lessons are available almost everywhere there are pools, beaches, lakes, rivers, oceans. Make sure the teacher is an expert—the Red Cross can help there!—and that he/she is understanding, patient, and will build the child's confidence.

Cheapest Outdoor Clothing and Equipment

Save up to 50 percent by making them yourself from a kit. There are many possibilities, from goosedown vests to full-size tents. The instructions are very specific, and there are quite a number of places which offer the kits for sale. If you are interested in checking out the catalogues, write to this "starter" group for theirs:
EMSKIT, Eastern Mountain Sports, 1041 Commonwealth Ave., Boston, Massachusetts 02215. Also: Mountain Sewn, Recreational Equipment, Inc., P.O. Box C-88125, Seattle, Washington 98188.

Safest Way to Drink Water

Strange cities, here and abroad, are not the only places where care must be taken with the drinking water. There is no guarantee of purity anywhere when hiking or camping out, so boil and even then drink sparingly.

The druggist or campers' supply store can provide water-sterilizing tablets as an alternative to boiling.

Fastest Way to Ski

Experts claim that you can ski fastest naked.

Cheapest Thrilling Winter Sport

If you thirst for exciting winter sport, but don't want to spend an arm and a leg to do it, try snurfing. The Snurfboard looks like a finless water ski with a tether rope attached to the front. It's inexpensive and can be found at most sporting goods stores or department store sport areas.

Learning to snurf is as easy as falling down. Find a hill, preferably a small one at first, and point the Snurfer downhill. Position your feet on the Snurfer, one behind the other, and with tether rope in hand, slide down the hill. If the snow is too sticky to allow a standing start, it helps to slide the Snurfer back and forth under your leading foot to clean the bottom, and then push off with your trailing foot. After a few days of this wonderful, cost-free sport, you may find yourself so busy having fun that you'll even give up skiing!

Fastest Way to Improve Your Golf Game

Use hot golfballs. Hot golfballs travel farther than those at normal temperatures and with a few warmed-up balls you can add distance to your drives immediately. The "Hotshot Golf Ball Booster" holds three golf balls and is designed to heat them right to the core. It will plug into any standard socket and is available from Hammacher Schlemmer, 145 East 57 Street, New York, New York 10019 for $19.95.

RESTAURANTS AND ENTERTAINMENT

Cheapest Way to Order in a Restaurant

Order a la carte—*and only what you want*. Remember, there's no law that says a meal has to consist of appetizer, soup, salad, entrée, and dessert. Most people order far more than they want or need in a restaurant, largely out of the mistaken assumption that for a meal to be a meal it has to include all of the above. In fact, in many restaurants just ordering the entrée will provide you with a vegetable or two automatically, and that may be more than enough. A bowl of soup and a salad may well make a satisfying meal. The important thing is to ask yourself what *you* want to eat, and not be intimidated, through either habit or the way menus are organized, into ordering more courses than you need.

Cheapest Time to Eat in an Expensive Restaurant

Many expensive restaurants have less expensive luncheon menus. By eating at noon rather than in the evening you can get the same high quality food and elegant atmosphere at much lower prices. Consider having your next meal out at lunch. It could save you a lot of money and allow you to sample the fare of a restaurant you couldn't have afforded in the evening. Many restaurants also have lower prices throughout the afternoon until some arbitrary time—often 5:00 or 5:30 P.M.—so that if you're willing to eat a little early you can even eat your evening meal at the lower prices.

Cheapest Nights for a Night on the Town

Many nightclubs and restaurants have lower prices in midweek than on weekends and raise their prices expressly for Saturday night. Check with your favorite nightspot. It may pay you to make your next traditional Saturday-night-out a Wednesday.

INDEX

Accountants fees, 204–5
Acne
  cheapest (and oldest) care, 2
  fastest care, 2
Adult education, information about, 156
Advertise, most effective way to, 161
Advice network, 186–87
African violets, 113, 115; 116
Age and aging, 2
Agriculture, U.S. Department of, 30, 125, 234, 237
Air-conditioner
  fan speed, most efficient, 81
  start-up temperature for, 80–81
Air-conditioning, cheapest, 81
Air-cooling device, most efficient, 80
Air fare, prepaying, 225
Air filter, furnace, 76
Air-layering, 113
Airline complaint hot-line, 228
Airport checkout, fastest, 227–28
Alarm systems, 90
Alcohol, 92
  rubbing, 93
  and sex, 3
Alimony settlement, 197–98
Allergy, common, 3
Aloe cactus, 15
Alternator, 87
Aluminum foil, 65
American Academy of Dermatology, 3
American Association of Retired Persons, 8, 204
American Bar Association, 153
American Indians, 127
American Kennel Club, 247
American Optometric Association, 9
Ammonia, 91, 93
Amtrak, 231
Angel food cake, 55

Animals and pests, 130–33
Aphid dip, 115–16
Aphrodisiac, 3
Appellate conferee, 221
Appetite, curbing, 26
Appetizer and digestive aid, 12
Applesauce
  fastest, 53
  healthiest, 52–53
Appliances, energy-saving, 67–69
Aquarium high water mark, 92–93
Assistance, governmental, 178
Aslan Clinic, 2
Asparagus, cooking, 46
Aspic, 39
Audit
  avoiding, 220
  handling of, 221
Auditor's findings, appealing, 221
Auto travel, 225
Avocado
  diced, 34
  ripening an, 53
Axle-grease stains, 92

Baby oil, 24
Baggage service, free, 231
Bags under eyes, getting rid of, 21
Baking sheet for cookies, 56
Baking soda, 92
Baldness, prevention of, 19
Ballpoint pen ink, stain from, 91
Bank Leu International Ltd., 184
Bankruptcy, 176–77
  calculating candidacy for, 176
  re-establishing credit after, 177
  retaining possessions during, 176
Banks, convenience or savings, 169

Basic Educational Opportunity Grants (BEOG), 147–48
  application, 149
  money for additional expenses, 148
Basic Grants, 148
Bathroom
  cleaning, 69
  energy saving, 70
Bathroom tile, refurbishing of, 101
Bathtub, cleaning, 69–70
Battery, 87
Bean sprouts, 109–10
Beans, 46–47
Beauty, top to toe, 17–27
Bed, glamor for, 101
Bedroom mirror, 101
Bee hives, 125
Bee sting, 14
Beeswax, 5
Beet tops, 125
Begonia, 135
Bequests, making, 200–1
Bird feeder, 247
Bird food
  cheapest, 248
  testing, 247–48
Black Russian, mintiest, 60
Blisters
  avoiding, 3
  relief from, 3
Blood flow, stopping, 3–4
Blood pressure, reducing, 4
Blood stains, 92
Boarders, 218
Boat-bus tour in northeast, 234
Body heat, raising, in winter, 11
Body lotion, 24
Bonds to save estate taxes, 203
Book(s)
  cheapest scholarly, 154–55
  hard-to-find, 154
Book store, cheapest, 155
Bookshelf space, 103–4
Boots, keeping women's in order, 95
Borax, 91, 92
Bottle tops, no stick, 98
Brands, house, 28–29

Bread, 36
  way to freshen, 36
Breathing, 4
Brick, stains on, 93
Britrail Pass, 243
Broccoli, cooking, 46
Broom handle, repair of, 99
Brown University, 144
Bulb(s)
  forcing, 112
  most energy-efficient, 81
  naturalizing of, 134
Burgers, easy forming, 41
Business expenses, 210–13
Business-pleasure trips, 220
Bustline, increasing, 22–23
Buying and selling, 162–66

Cabbage
  Chinese, 51
  stop smell of, 47
Cabbage butterfly, 131
Cabbage worms, 130
Cadmium, and blood pressure, 4
Caffeine, 4
Cake
  angel food, 55
  decorating, 55
  prevent sticking of, 55
  red and white baking brick, 55
Camphor, spirits of, 92
Can, opening a, 31
Candle wax drippings, 93
Candy, sugar-free, 57
Capitol Switchboard, 194
Car, 85–88
  divesting yourself of a "lemon," 194
  non-starting, 87
Car trade-in, best time for, 165
Cardboard cartons, 66
Career adventure, 152–61
Carpet, stains on, 91
Carrots, planting, 126
Cash
  counting, 168
  stash of, 90
Cast-iron plant (aspidistra), 110
Casualty and theft losses, 217–18

Cavitron, 6

Celery and endive, blanching, 126

Chapped lips, 5

Charge account debt, cheapest way to settle, 174–75

Charity, 216

Check(s), 169–71
  dates, verification of, 206
  do-it-yourself, 170
  protecting, 169

Checks on money fund, writing, 170

Cheese grater, 66

Chewing gum, removal of, 92

Child care, 217–18
  expenses, reducing, 217

Chlorophyll, 6–7

Cholesterol, 5

Christmas, 104–6
  gift wrapping, 104
  motif, 105–6
  presents, time to buy, 167

Christmas tree
  care and safety, 106
  recycling, 121

Christmas wraps, tips for, 105–6

Chronicle of Higher Education, 154

Cigarette odor, removal of, 70

Cigarette stains on marble, removal of, 93

Cigars, best way to buy, 212

Citizen's arrests, 197

Civil Aeronautics Board, Office of Consumer Advocate at, 228

Clearinghouse on Adult Education and Life-Long Learning, 156

Clothes
  care of, 26, 95–96
  pressing, 229

Clothes drying
  more effective, 72
  most efficient, 72

Cocktail-mixing books, free, 58

Cocktail substitute, 63–64

Cocktails on flights, cheapest, 226

Codicil, 200

Coffee
  lift from, 63
  stains, 92

Coins, 239

Cola syrup, 13

Cold frames, 124

Cole slaw, 50

Collards, 126

College
  financial help, 146–53
  getting into, 143–45
  least expensive, 153

College campus copier, 167–68

College-education fund, 202

College Scholarship Service (CSS), 146

College teachers salaries, 160

College Venture Program, 158

College-Work Study Program (CWS), 149

Commerce, U.S. Department of, 163

Community health center, and psychiatric care, 8

Company car, 212

Composting, 120

Concrete patio, freshening, 104

Condensation in basement, 82

Congressional representative, reaching your, 193–94

Consumer(s)
  complaint process, 193
  information, 162
  rights, 193–94

Consumer Affairs, Office of, 29

Consumer Information Center, 162, 191

Consumer Product Safety Commission, 86, 194

Consumer Reports, 162

Contact lenses, hard or soft, 9

Contingency fees, 197

Cookery, speed-up, 40

Cookies
  baking sheet for, 56
  home-baked, 56
  patterned, 56

Cooking
  energy saving, 68
  information, 31–32
  time, 32

Cooling, 79–81

Cooling a house, cheapest way to, 79–80
Copper, and allergies, 3
Corn, 126
  plastic mulch for, 127
Corn earworms, 131
Corner desk, 102
Cottage cheese, 34
Council on International Educational Exchange, 236
Counterfeit bills, test for, 168
Coupons, clipping, 163
Court system, most efficient, 195
Cousteau Society, 160
Cover crops, 120
Crabgrass, 138
Credit, 171–73
  tips about, 171
Credit card protection, 173
Credit counselors, cheapest, 171
Credit history, ways to build, 171–72
Credit rating
  correcting, 172
  improving, 172–73
Credit union, 174
Creeping charley, 114
Cress, 108–9
Crocus, 134
Crystal decanter, removal of film from, 94
Cucumber alert, 50
Cut flowers, long-lasting, 107
Cutworm bait, 131
Cutworm collar, 131

Dampness, causes of, 82
Dandelion(s), 47, 138
Dandelion greens, harvesting, 47
Dandruff, preventing, 5
Deaf taxpayers, 204
Decorating, 101–4
Decorator look, 100
Decorator-tips, 99–104
Dental care
  cheapest, 6
  most efficient, 6
Deodorant, 6–7
Depositing monthly government checks, 178–79

Depression and hot weather, 5
Derriere, flatter, 23
Destination
  learning about, 223
  researching your, 235
Dimmer light switches, 82
Dip, quick, 38
Direct deposit, 178
Direct Mail Marketing Association, 85
Disaster, way to minimize, 217
Disbudding, 134
Dishes
  drying, 69
  stains on, 91
Distilled water, cheapest, 77
Divorce-related tax advantage, 217
Divorce Yourself, 196
Do-it-yourself repairs, 96–101
Doctor
  finding a, 7
  in foreign country, 237
Dog, learning about, 247
Dollars, exchanging, 238–39
Doorway, 100
Double chin, concealing, 22
Drafts, reducing, 78
Draperies, and energy, 77
Drawers, unsticking, 97
Dried flower arrangement, 108
Drink(s), 58–64
  blender, 60
  chill bottled, 59
  serving at cocktail party, 60
  summer slices for, 59
  twist for, 59
Driver's license, as identification, 89
Drugs
  cheapest, 8
  discounts for those over 55, 8
Dryer
  cheapest, 72
  cheapest load for, 72
  most efficient use of, 72
Dying plant, 114–15

Ear infection, and swimming, 9
Earthwatch, 235
Eastern Air-Shuttle, 231

Education, U.S. Office of, 147, 148, 149, 150, 151
Education and career, 139–61
Egg(s)
    boil without breaking, 33
    cheapest, 33
    grade of, 32–33
    hard-boiled, 33
    low cost, 33
    peeling hard-boiled, 33
    poaching, 35
    quickest way to cook, 33
    separating, 35
Egg treat, baked, 34
Egg white, 92
Elbow roughness, eliminating, 23
Elderly people, temperatures for, 74
Electric iron, removing scratches from, 73
Electric wiring, inspecting, 89
Eligibility Index Formula, computation of, 148
Eligibility index number, 148
Embroidered linens, ironing, 74
Emergency(ies)
    phone list, 89
    preparation for, 89
Emergency call, anticipating, 223–24
Employment agency, fastest service by, 157
Emskit, 250
Encyclopedia of Associations, 31, 154
Energy
    cost cutters, 74–75
    and tax savings, 214
Energy, Department of, 68, 95
Entertainment on board, 226–27
Equal Credit Opportunity Act, 171, 173
Estate planning
    considerations in, 198
    and wills, 198–201
Estate taxes, reducing, 203
Eurail pass, 242–43
Europe
    cheapest flight to, 237–38
    low rates for flying around, 242

    traveling around, 243
Exemption
    claiming a parent as, 207
    double, 207
Exercise
    and appetite, 26
    cheapest, 25
    gardener's, 26
    most efficient, 25
    water, 25–26
    while flying, 227
Exercise mat, 25
Experiment in International Living, 159
Eye puffiness, ending, 20–21
Eyelash(es)
    lengthener, 21
    thicker, 21
Eyes, bags under, 21

Face lift, 21
Facial
    cheapest, 19–20
    exercise, 19
    kitchen, 20
Fair Credit Reporting Act, 172
Fan
    attic, 80
    whole-house ventilating, 80
Fare between two points, cheapest, 225
Fat, eliminate from soup, 37
Federal Crime Insurance, 182
Federal Highway Administration, 167
Federal Housing Administration, 89
Federal Trade Commission, 143, 180
Fennel, 13
Financial Aid Form (FAF), 146
Finger, saving severed, 3–4
Fingernails, keeping clean, 98
Fire escape plans, 89–90
Fireplace, most efficient use of, 78–79
Fireplace damper, 79
    how to unstick, 79
First Aid kits, 225–26
First National Bank of Chicago, 186

Fish
  baking, 39
  coating, for frying, 40—41
  way to sweeten, 39
Flatulence, reducing, 12
Flea beetles, 131
Floodlights, reflector, 81
Floor, cheapest way to cover, 101
Floor plan, most energy-efficient, 78
Flower(s), 133—35
  arrangement, 108
  cut and dried, 108
  dried, 108
  perennial, 133
  pest-free, 135
  pinching back, 135—36
Flower bonds, 203
Food(s)
  canned, 30, 31
  and drink, 38
  economical way to buy, 29
  green, 47
  locating unusual, 31
  party, 51
  slicing at home, 31
Food cooler, 32
Food dryer, build your own, 110
Food-shopping schedule, 30—31
Foot comfort, 227
  in summer, 10
Foot moisturizer, 23
Foot problems, preventing, 10
Foreign currency, 238
Foreign language
  cheapest way to learn, 155
  fastest way to learn, 155—56
Forsythia branches, 136
Foster care, 216
Freckle remedy, 20
Freezer temperature, 67—68
Freezers, storage, 68
Freezing weather, dressing for, 11
Freshener or toner, 20
Frostbite, preventing, 11
Fruit(s)
  bird-proof, 211
  and fruit desserts, 52—55
  stains, 92
  and vegetables, 125—30

Fruit trees, dwarf, 135
Furnace, energy-saving for, 77—78
Furniture, scratches in, 94

Garage sale, 168
Garbage disposal
  keeping fresh, 66
  water temperature for, 69
Garden tools, protecting, 119
Gardener's friend, 137
Gardening
  container, 118—19
  intensive, 117—18
Garlic, aging, 50
Gas stove, ignition for, 69
Gasoline
  saving on, 85
  in trunk, 86
  use, most efficient, 86
Generic drugs, 8
Generic foods, 28—29
Gerovital HS, 2
Getting to work, cheapest way to, 212
Gift(s), 166—67
  best buys, 166
  cheapest, 166—67, 243
  for home, 243—44
Ginseng, 3
Glass(es)
  chilling, 59
  cocktail, 59
  efficient cleaner, 9
  frosted, 59
Glitter, evening, 27
Glycerine, 92
Gold, 184—186
  way to invest in, 185—86
Gold coin(s)
  cheapest, 185—86
  fastest way to buy, 186
Gold Deposit Certificate, 184
Gold leaf frame, polishing of, 94
Golden Age Passport, 235
Golden Eagle Passport, 234, 235
Golf game, improving your, 251
Gopher-proof garden, 131—32
Gotu kola, 13

Gourmet, 223
Government interest, 219
Government Printing Office, 125, 235
Graduate Equivalency Diploma (GED), 143–44
Graduate school, free tuition at, 152–53
Grapes, frosted, 53
Grass stains, 92
Grasshopper, 60
Grater, cleaning, 66
Gravies, fat-free, 43
Greenhouse, build your own, 116
Growing season, extending, 118
"GSP and the Traveler," 237
Guaranteed Student Loan Program (GSL), 151
Guest room tips, 103
Guitar, buying a, 248
Guitar strings, stretching life of, 249
Guns, in home, 90–91

Hair
  brushing, 18
  care schedule, 17
  conditioners, 19
  setting lotion, 19
  tips about, 17–18
Hairdo, fastest, 18
Hambone, art of, 249
Hands, dishpan, end to, 23
Handy-wipes, 65
Hangers, slip-proof, 95
Hangover
  cheapest cure for, 11
  fastest cure for, 11
  practical cure for, 11–12
Hash, frying, 42
Health Education Assistance Loan (HEAL), 151–52
Health insurance, 179
  group, 179
Healthy, how to stay, 1
Heating, 76–79
Heating and cooling, general, 74–76
Heat pump system, 75
Herb garden, window sill, 108

Herbs, 108–9
  drying and storing, 109
Hiccups, cure for, 12
High school diploma, 142–43
Hinge, oiling, 97
Hive remedy, 12
Hobby, use of, 212–13
Holiday, 223
Hollandaise, 38
Home
  dressing up, 100
  heating aid, cheapest, 77
  safety, 88–91
Home fries, 44
Home office deduction, 220
Home slicing, 31
Homework, efficient order for, 141
Hosiery, 26
Hospital, best time to enter, 7
Hot beds, 124
Hot caps, 124
  instant, 124
Hot weather and depression, 5
Hotel Cluny, 240
Hotplate, stains on, 92
House
  guidelines for buying, 165–66
  selling your, 166
  stretching use of, 99
House identification, 88
House plant(s), 110–15
  humid, 111–12
  most durable, 110–11
  rejuvenation, 115
House-sale losses, 214–15
Hypothermia, risk of, 74

Ice cream, 5
Ice cream sodas, nourishing, 56
Icelandic Airlines, 238–39
Icing, 56
Income for college, supplemental, 152
Income scrutinizing, 206
Income tax savings, health-related, 210
Indigestion relief, 12
Indoor gardening, 107–16
Indoor slate, 95
Insomnia, cure for, 12
Instant-on TV, operating, 246

Insurance(s), 179–82
  claim, settlement of, 182
  disability, 213
  government, 182
  investment, most efficient, 180
  payment schedule, 181
  term, 179
Insure, quickest way to, 181–82
Interest
  deductible, 216
  tax-free, 216
Interest rates, taking advantage of, 182–83
Interior, U.S. Department of, 234, 235
International Air Transport Association (IATA), 182–83
International Association for Medical Assistance to Travelers, 237
International Home Exchange Service, 229
International Publications, 159
Interservice Home Exchange, 229
Investing, 182–84
Iodine, 94
Ireland, 236
Irish Union of Students, 236
Iron cross begonias, 113
Ironing
  dampening clothes for, 73
  most efficient, 73
IRS audit, 219–21
Ivy League education, 144–45
Ivy League school, 144

Jade, 116
Japanese beetle traps, 132
Jewelry
  costume, 3
  protecting, 224
Jiffy-7 pellets, 123
Job(s), 156–58
  advice, free, 156–57
  best time to look for, 157
  in Britain, 159–60
  fastest way to get, 157
  looking for, 157, 210–11
  overseas, 159

  summer, 158
  while taking time off from college, 158
Journal of Commerce, 181
Jumprope, 25
Junk mail
  how to stop, 85
  source of, 84
Justice, fastest path to, 197

Kerosene space heater, 78
Kids, tags for, 230
Kitchen tips, 65–66
Knife, cleaning, 66
Knitting wool, moth-free, 96

Labor, Department of, 157
Laker Airways, 238
Laker Travel Center, 238
Landscaping, and energy savings, 137–38
Large items, cheapest way to buy, 164
Late payments, capitalizing on, 219
Laundry
  saving energy, 72
  sweet-smelling, 71
Laundry detergent, economy in, 71
Laundry room, 70–71
  energy saving, 71–74
Law, 192–201
Law school, cheapest way to go to, 153–54
Lawn, 138
  mowing, 138
  watering time, 138
Lawyer
  cheapest, 196
  fastest way to find, 195
  and lawsuits, 195–97
Layering, 136
Leaf cuttings, 113
Leaf sections, 113–14
Leaf-vein cuttings, 113
Learning on your own, 154–56
Lease(s), 192–93
  breaking, 193
  most efficient, 192–93

Leftovers
    nutritional, 52
    use of, 52
Legal Aid Society, 196
Legal arrangement, 196–97
Legal fees, 196, 221
Legal insurance, 196
Legal services, incompetent,
    196
Lemonade, pinkest spiked, 60
Lemons
    best ideas for, 53–54
    buying, 53
Letter of Instruction, 199–200
Lettuce, drying, 50
Life insurance, 179–81
    borrowing against, 174
    cheapest, 179
    shopping for, 180–81
Light, 81–82
Light switch, most efficient, 82
Lighting, most efficient, 81
Lighting costs, reducing, 81–82
Lima beans, 127
Linen closets, tips for, 102
Linen tablecloth, ironing, 73–
    74
Linton Yield, 180
Lipstick repair, 22
Loan, cheapest, 174
Loans and debts, 174–76
Lodging
    cheap, 228–29
    in Europe, cheapest, 239–40
Log carrier, cheapest, 79
London, cheapest way to fly,
    238
London to Edinburgh, cheapest
    way, 242
Long-distance calls, 164
Long flight, preparing for, 226
Lopsided plant, treatment for,
    111
Louvered doors and windows,
    80
Lowell National Historical Park,
    234
Lunch, elegant, 34

Mail, protecting, 169–70
Makeup, setting, 20
Mantis egg cases, 133

Maps, 231
Marijuana, and sex, 3
Marinating, 41
Marine biology, 160
Marriage, ending a, 197–98
marshmallows, cutting, 56
Martindale-Hubbell Lawyer's
    Dictionary, 195
Massage, quick, 19
Master Charge, 172
Mealy bugs, cure for, 116
Meat
    buying, 39–40
    coating for frying, 40–41
    flavoring, tips for, 41
Meat or bread boards, stains
    on, 91
Meat pie, 42
Meatloaf tips, 42
Medicaid information, 7
Medical costs, deducting, 206
Medical resource, cheapest, 8–9
Medical school, 145
Memorize, most efficient way
    to, 141
Men
    best shave for, 27
    specially for, 27
Menstrual cramps, relieving, 13
Mice control, 83
Mildew treatment, 93–94
Mileage, 86
Military uniforms, deductions
    for, 213
Milk, way to keep longer, 35
Mites, washing off, 115
Moldings, 100
Monetary gifts, distribution of,
    203
Money, 162–91
    and banking, 168–69
    getting more for your, 30
    interest-free, 174
    keeping it straight, 239
Money orders, cheapest, 169
Mortgage loans, advantages of
    secondary, 175
Mountain Sewn, 250
Mouse traps, 83
Mouthwash, natural, 13
Move, cheapest way to, 211

Mulch
  newspaper, 121
  plastic, 121
Mushrooms, 34
  slicing, 47
  stuffed, 47
Musical instrument, cheapest, 249

Nail care, 23
Nailing, 97–98
Narcissus, 134
National Consumer Buying Alert, 162
National Council of Senior Citizens, 204
National Direct Student Loan (NDSL), 150
National Fire Protection Association, 89
National Foundation for Consumer Credit, 171
National Park Service, 158, 234, 235
National parks, entree to, 234
National Science Foundation, 88
Nausea, relieving, 13
Negative income tax, 178
New books, cheapest, 154
New York Times, 155
Newspaper, getting your name in, 161
Nickel, and allergies, 3
Night cream, 24
Night on the town, 252
Nitrogen, leafy vegetables and, 119
Nose job, 22
Nosebleeds, stopping, 13
Note taking, 140

Obscene telephone calls, 84
Octane rating, best, 85
Oil and gas lottery, 191
Oil furnace
  checking efficiency of, 76
  modification, 76
Omelet, 34
  professional, 34
Onions
  peeling, 48
  without tears, 48

Opthamologist, 10
Optician, 10
Optometrist, 10
Orange, peeling an, 54
Orange juice, freshest-tasting, 64
Outdoor clothing and equipment, 250
Outdoor gardening, 117–38
  garden planning, 117–19
  seeds and transplanting, 121–24
  soil, 119–21
Outdoors, 249–51
Oven cleaning, 66
Oveseas news in English, 156
Overseas telephone calls, 84
Oxford, 145

Package contents, 30
Paint stains on glass, 92
Paint thinner, 93
Paintbrush, keeping soft, 97
Painted walls, custom-look, 100
Painting, spot-free, 96–97
Pancakes, painless, 36
Paper, pack your own, 224
Paris
  best cheap hotel in, 240
  getting around, 240–41
Parsley, 7, 50, 108
Party food, healthiest, 51
Pasta
  elegant, 43–44
  keep from sticking, 43
Payments, inability to meet, 175–76
Pea brush, 127
Peas
  dried, 48
  split, 48
  whole, 48
Peperomia, 113
Pepper plants, 127
Pepper-uppers for summer, low calorie, 63
Peppers, freezing, 128
Perennials, dividing, 134
Perfume
  cheapest, 24
  choosing, 24–25
Persimmon, ripening a, 54

Personnel Management, Office of, 157
Perspiration stains, 91
Pests
  birds and, 133
  rodents and, 83–84
Petroleum jelly, 24, 93
  and ear infection, 9
  and skin wrinkling, 24
Pets, 246–48
Philadelphia, cheapest way to get around, 233
Philodendron, 114
Phone and mail, 84–85
Phonograph records, cleaning and restoring, 94
Picture windows, 90
Pineapple, growing your own, 112
Pineapple and strawberries St. Teresa, 54–55
Pipes, rattling, 98
Pitch or tar stains, 91–92
Placemats, 103
Plant bugs and pests, 115–16
Plant lights, 111
Plants, hybrid, 121–22
Plastic stretch wrap, 66
Plastic wrappers, 163–64
Poinsettia, forcing into bloom, 112
Poison ivy
  emergency treatment, 13
Polident, 91
Pollination, 135
Popcorn, 57
Popcorn balls, 57
Porcelain stains, 70
Pork
  economy, 42
  high quality, 42
Possessions, arrangement of, 103
Postum, as coffee substitute, 4
Potassium fertilizer, 120
Potatoes
  baked, 44
  breakfast or supper casserole, 46
  for entree, 45
  hash browned, 44
  low-calorie treat, 45

  mashed, 45
  oven-fried, 45
  patties, 46
  peelings, 45
  reuse baked, 44
  scalloped, 45
  serving, 45–46
Poultry
  buys, 40
  coating, for frying, 40–41
Pounds, keeping off, 39
Power of attorney, 199
Preparation H, 21
Preservative, old-fashioned, 35
Procrastination, 140
Product safety, 194
Product Safety Commission, 194
Property taxes, appealing, 215–16
Psychiatric care, cheapest, 8
Psychiatrists and psychologists, distinction between, 8
Publications, low cost, 125

Rabbit repellant, 132
Rabbits, 132
Radiators, 77
Raincoat, 27
Rainy weather, preparing for, 224
Rapid transit fares, 233
Rats, getting rid of, 83–84
Real estate appraisal, 165
Real estate deduction, 214
Real estate taxes, 215
Recipe file, 32
Recreation, 242–52
Refrigerator
  location, 67
  most efficient, 67
  reducing operating costs, 67
Refrigerator door, checking seal on, 67
Relax, cheapest way to, 15
Religious freaks, 226
Renting, 167
Restaurant(s)
  cheapest time to eat in expensive, 252
  and entertainment, 251–52
  ordering in, 251–52

Restaurant guide, U.S., 233–34
Restaurant meals, 241
Retirement, preparation for, 203
Rex begonias, 113
Rolls, way to freshen, 36
Room(s)
    making it cosy, 99
    to unify, 99
Room decor, most energy-efficient, 77
Room fragrance, 70
Root crops, storage, 125
Root maggot, 132–33
Round shoulders, cure for, 22
Rubber gloves, 98
Running in sand, 249
Running shoes, 249
Rust stains, 91

Salad(s)
    best ideas, 51–52
    preservation tip, 50
Salad garden, basement, 109
Sales, supermarket, 28
Sales-tax deductions, increasing, 213–14
Salt-seltzer, 12
Sandpaper, 98
Sandwich, packing a, 36
Savings, 167–68
    for a treat, 167
Savings bank life insurance, 179
Scarecrow, 130
Scholarship
    obtaining, 146–47
    for out-of-state colleges, 149–50
Scholarship information, federal, 147
Scholastic Aptitude Test, 144–45
School(s)
    best, 141–42
    cheapest private, 142
School and college, 141–42
Scissors, sharpening, 99
Scratch paper, 85
Screw, loose, 97
Seasonings, 50
Security deposit, 209

Seed(s)
    old, 122
    sowing small, 123
    starting, 123–24
    storage, 122
Seed starter, indoor, 122
Seedling, thinning of, 123
Self organization, 139
Senior citizen super-savers, 341
Setting lotion, 19
Severed finger, 3–4
Sewing, 96
    kits, 224
Shade trees, most efficient use of, 76
Shampoo, dry, 18
Shampoo stretcher, 18
Shave, best for men, 27
Sheets, identifying size of, 71
Shoepolish, liquid, 94
Shoes
    for everyday, 10
    for women, 10–11
Shopping, 28–31
    cheapest, 237
    efficiently, 28–29
    by mail, 163
    planning ahead for, 225
Shower, energy saving, 70
Shrubs, full looking, 136
Sights, U.S., 234–35
Silicone lubricant, 97
Sinuses, clearing, 14
Ski, fastest way to, 250
Skin
    itchy and dry, 23–24
    preventing from wrinkling in bathtub, 24
Sleeping quarters, 228
Sleeve length, 27
Small claims court, 193
Smoke, 88–89
Smoke detector, 88
Snail bait, 132
Snapdragon seeds, refrigeration of, 133–34
Sneeze prevention, 14
Snow, 137
Soap saver, 22
Social security, 177–79
    way to get, 177–78

Social Security Administration, 177

Socks, sorting, 70–71

Soft-sided luggage, packing, 224

Soil, sterilizing, 114

Sore throat, cure for, 5

Soup(s)
  best, 36
  canned, 38
  cold, 38
  cream of tomato, 37
  eliminate fat from, 37
  fastest, 37
  green, 37
  unsalt, 38

Soup stock, 37

South wall, plant near, 118

Souvenirs, 243–44

Special services, 231

Spinach
  early, 128
  frozen, 37
  hot weather, 128
  removing water from boiled, 48

Splatter, stopping, 41

Splinter remover, 14

Squash, winter, 128

Stains. See also specific stain
  and cleaning, 91–95
  porcelain, 70

Stanley Kaplan Testing Agency, 143

Steam iron, unplugging holes in, 73

Stem cuttings, 114

Stocks, 186–91
  cheapest way to invest in number, 187–88
  leverage on, 188–90
  leverage on falling, 190
  making money on falling, 190

Stock market advice, 186–87

Stock market reports, 186

Stocks and bonds, safest way to keep, 187

Stopping for the night, 232

Strawberries, weeding, 128–29

Strawberry jam, 55

Stress reliever, 15

Student Air Travel Association, 242

Student Eligibility Report (SER), 148

Student loans, 150

Student traveling abroad, benefits for, 236

Study, most efficient way to, 140–41

Study habits, 140–41

Stuffing shortcuts, 36

Success, shortcuts to, 139–40

Summer courses, 142

Sun and gardening, 117

Sunburn lotion, 15

Sunburn remedy, 15

Sunglass test, 9

Sunny buds, 111

Supplementary Educational Opportunity Grant (SEOG), 149

Swedish ivy, 114

Swimming
  and ear infection, 9
  lessons for children, 250
  and stress relief, 15

Swiss chard, 48–49
  cooking, 46, 49
  use in salads, 49

Swiss franc bank account, 183–84

Table, cover for, 103

Tartar, cream of, 91

Tax(es), 202–22
  best time to itemize, 205–6
  business deductions, 211
  cheapest large city for, 203–4
  credit, 209
  deductible, 213–14
  exemptions, 207–10
  filing extensions, 218
  high singles rate, 208–9
  homeowner's deductions, 214–16
  parental exemptions, 208
  strategy, 206–7
  tax-free, 213

Tax audit advice, 220

Tax court, 221

Tax-exempt bonds, 220

Tax-free home sale, 214

Tax information, 204
   for the aged, 204
Tax preparation, 204–6
   avoiding fraud, 205
Tax preparers
   cheapest, 205
   finding, 205
Tax records, 219
Tax regulations, parental, 207–8
Tax returns, old, 219
Tax sales, prevention of, 215
Taxpayer Service Division, 204
Tea
   pink lemon, 63
   pink mint, 63
   rose hip, 63
Tea bags, cheapest, 63
Tea stains, 92
Teeth-cleaning device, fastest, 6
Telephone calls, 239
   from airport, 228
Teleservice, 177
Tension, relief of, 15
Test scores, standardized, 143–44
Theft loss, way to corroborate, 216–17
Thermostat
   and house plants, 110
   location of, 74
   settings, most efficient, 74
Time deposits, early withdrawal, 209
Tin, and allergies, 3
Tires, most efficient, 86
Toilet, most efficient, 70
Tomato(es), 129–30
   cages, 129
   cherry, 34
   peeling, 49
   ripening, 49, 130
Tomato plant, 129
   tall, 129–30
Tomato sauce, homemade, 38
Tomato soup, uncurdled cream of, 37
Tool, handiest, 224
Tooth powder, 16
Tooth reimplantation, 6
Toothpaste, 16

Trailer, 228–29
Transplants, timing of, 118, 123
Transportation, Department of, 85
Transportation in towns, 241
Travel
   abroad, 235–37
   basics, 223–28
   between New York and Washington (or Boston), 231–32
   information, 230
   long-distance, 230–31
   and tourism, 223–44
Travel and Leisure, 223
Travel tips, U.S., 233–34
Travelers' checks, place to cash, 239
"Travelers Tips," 237
Traveling photographer, 225
Travellers' insurance, 226
Tree(s)
   protecting trunks, 137
   and shrubs, 135
   watering newly planted, 135
Trisodium phosphate, 93
Trust, establishing a, 201
Tuition fees, tax deductible, 152
Turkey, 42–43
Turpentine, 92
TV antenna, adjusting, 245–46
TV watching, 245

Undergraduate Rule of Thumb, 146
Undergraduate students, federal loans for part-time, 151
United Buying Service, 164
University of California Extension, 145
Unlisted phones, 84
Unpacking, 229
USA Travel Information Center, 230

Vacation Exchange Club, 229
Vacation home, 215, 229
Vacations, inexpensive, 235–36

Valuables, safe-keeping place for, 90
Value Line Investment Survey, 187
Vegetable(s), 110–11
  cooking, 46
  growing, 125–28
  liquid from cooked, 46
  winter, 109
Ventilation, natural, 80–81
Vestibule, 78
Veterans, free college tuition for, 150
Veterans Administration Educational Benefits, (VETS), 150
Vinegar, 92, 94
  and rooting, 114
  white, 91
Vision aid, for over 60, 9
Vitamin, quickest shot, 46
Vitamin-laced drink, 46
Vodka, coldest, 60
Vodka drink, pinkest, 60–61

Walking, 25
Wall Street Journal, 188
Wandering jew, 114
Washer load size, most efficient, 71
Watch repairs, capitalizing cost of, 212
Water, 82–83
  and health, 8–9
  room for, 114
  safest way to drink, 250
Water spots, removal of, 93
Watering, 119
Watermelons, quick, 130
Waterproof, basement, 83
Wave Project, 196

Wax build-up on furniture, 93
Weatherization, cheapest, 75
Weatherization assistance program, 75
Wedding dissolution, 198
Weeds, 119–20
Weekend vacation, 232
Wildflowers, gathering, 107
Will
  most efficient, 199
  place to keep, 200
  updating, 200
Willow tree, planting, 136
Window(s)
  caulking, 75
  cleaning, 95
  locations, energy efficient, 75–76
Wine, 61–62
  breathing, 62
  buying, 61
  imported, 61
  pinkest white, 62
  storage, efficient, 61–62
Winter injury, preventing, 137–38
Winter warmup, low calorie, 63
Winter sport, cheapest thrilling, 251
Wiring money, 168–69
Witch hazel, 20
Women and credit, 173
Wrinkle remover, 95
Wrinkles, minimizing, 229
Writer, becoming a good, 141

Zinc
  and allergies, 3
  and blood pressure, 4
  and dandruff, 5
Zucchini, 34

CONTRIBUTORS

Major Contributors

Diana Adams is a freelance writer whose articles have appeared in many publications, including *The New York Times*, *Publisher's Weekly*, *Snack Foods Magazine* and *Jetaway*. She formerly worked in public relations as creative director of Ciangio-Mehlich and as vice president of Fujita Design, a subsidiary of Ruder & Finn in New York City. She is presently the owner and manager of The Pastry Garden, Inc., a bakery in Poughkeepsie, New York.

R. Mark Adams grew up on a fruit and vegetable farm in upstate New York. He studied agriculture at Cornell University and is currently the owner-operator of a 40,000-square-foot greenhouse operation.

Raina Grossman is an associate editor at United Feature Syndicate and a syndicated writer whose columns on television and TV personality profiles appear in several hundred U.S. newspapers. She has also published feature articles in the *New York Daily News*.

Michael Kronenwetter was a television critic, feature writer and book reviewer for the *Whig-Standard* (Ontario, Canada) for three years. He is the author of short stories, educational filmstrips and plays, and he is now writing and researching *The Illustrated Encyclopedia of World Dates and Events*, to be published by Facts on File.

Geraldine Merken lives in Massachusetts, where she divides her free time between a vegetable garden and a rock garden. She was a writer-editor for NBC-TV and WOR-TV for ten years and her articles have appeared in the *Christian Science Monitor*, *Ford Times*, *Buyways* and *Airfair*.

Joanna Walsh O'Neill is a New York-based freelance writer. Her short stories, celebrity interviews, reviews and criticism have appeared in *Seventeen*, *Co-Ed*, *Dance Scope*, *Television Quarterly* and other publications. Formerly the nationally syndicated film critic for cable TV network, Ms. O'Neill has hosted her own TV talkshow, "Dance, New York Style." She also conducted writing workshops at New York University for more than seven years.

Seymour Roman, a former newspaperman and long-time motion picture press agent, has no use for shortcuts in the enjoyment of two of his favorite activities. He does not speed-read, and he does his two-finger typing on an aged, non-electric portable. In his spare time, he writes for or about puppets.

Harry Shreiner is the author of *A Tribute to the King Elvis*. He has been an editor of various business journals and has written articles for *Coronet* and *Magazine Digest* among others.

Richard Trubo is the author of four books: *An Act of Mercy*, Nash, 1973; *The Insurance Handbook*, Doubleday, 1975; *How to Get a Night's Sleep*, Little, Brown, 1978; and *Hurting*, Simon & Schuster, 1978. His articles have appeared in many newspapers and magazines, including *TV Guide*, *Family Weekly*, *Parade*, TWA's *Ambassador*, the *Los Angeles Times*, and the *Chicago Tribune*, and he was a contributor to *The People's Almanac*® and *The Book of Lists*.

Other Contributors

Michael Antonoff is articles editor of *Genesis* magazine. He was formerly associate editor of *Moneysworth*, where he wrote the "Dollars & Sense" column, and a reporter at the *Bergen Record*. Articles of his have also appeared in *The New York Times*.

Louis Botto has been an editor of *Look*, *Interiors* and *Homelife* magazines. He is now associate editor of *Playbill*. His articles have appeared in *The New York Times Sunday Magazine*, *Ladies' Home Journal*, *People*, *American Home*, *Reader's Digest* and other national publications.

Din Dayal was formerly with the United Nations as an international training expert (International Labor Organization, Geneva). He is regional director of the North Jersey Greenthumb Program, a placement agency for senior citizens. He is also a professional engineer. He has published articles in numerous world publications, including the *Deccan Herald*, Banglore, India; *Pioneer*, Accra, Ghana; and the *Bergen County Record*.

David Gilman is a graduate of Lafayette College and a freelance writer living in New York. He is also a composer of recorded rock n' roll music for the Tommy Tutone Band.

Niels Johannesen is a freelance writer and a gardener. He has a roofing and siding business in Connecticut.

Donald B. Lane has been a management consultant and was a stockbroker for twenty years. He now writes for various publications and is a director of a west coast publishing company.

Bill Linn is a freelance writer who received a CAPS (Creative Artist's Public Service) grant for 1979. He has a Ph.D. in English from New York University and has taught at N.Y.U., Hunter and Brooklyn College. He has also published numerous articles and is writing a novel about Vietnam.

Robert Linn is a graduate of Brown University, an editor and education writer for the *Orlando Sentinel Star* (Orlando, Florida) as well as a freelance editor. He has contributed articles to the *Pittsburgh Post-Gazette* and the *Providence Journal Bulletin*. He has studied and worked in Europe.

Ann Michell, who has an M.A. in Consumer Studies and is a registered representative with the New York Stock Exchange, is a writer specializing in personal finance and related consumer topics. Her articles have appeared in *The New York Times, Redbook, Firehouse Magazine* and *Factoring and Finance Journal*, among others. She was formerly associate editor of *Consumer Gazette Magazine* and producer and moderator of the "Consumer Gazette of the Air," a weekly news and interview program on WNBC AM/FM radio.

Stephen A. Stertz has a Ph.D. in history from the University of Michigan and has published numerous scholarly articles in his field. He is now a researcher for the Bronx County Historical Society and does much freelance writing, editing and research.

CONSULTING EDITORS

Amy Greene, a former model, was a beauty editor for *Glamour* and *McCall's* magazines and a Fellow for Life of the Costume Institute of the Metropolitan Museum of Art. She has appeared a number of times on the "Best Dressed" list and is now president of Beauty Checkers, Inc., a small cosmetics firm specializing in "make-overs."

Michael Manley, a graduate of Georgetown University's School of Language and Linguistics, lived, studied and traveled in Europe for over ten years. A former travel agent, he is now a simultaneous translator specializing in English, French and German.

Jim Powell operates Heritage Park Restaurant located in an historic Victorian house in San Diego, California and helped to found other restaurants. He has traveled extensively in Europe, the United States and North Africa.

Nick Powell has been owner, manager and chef of three restaurants and bars in Park City and Salt Lake City, Utah. He is a connoisseur of various ethnic foods, having dined well, if not always wisely, throughout the United States, western and eastern Europe, and North Africa.

Kathi Wakefield, who holds a Masters Degree in business administration, is the founder of MORE for WOMEN, Inc., a career counseling service.

TO OUR READERS
FUTURE EDITIONS

If reading these pages has reminded you of old shortcuts of your own or stimulated you to invent new ones,
we hope that you will contribute them to our future
SHORTCUTS books. The editors will pay you a one-
time fee of 10¢ a published word for any contribution
that is published. You will also receive a contributor's
by-line if more than five of your contributions are published. Send your shortcuts along with the signed form
below to:

> THE EDITORS OF SHORTCUTS
> c/o Superlative House, Inc.
> P.O. Box 888, FDR Station
> New York, New York 10022

Allow at least three to six months for a response.
Do not address inquires to Bantam Books.

— — — — — — — — — — — — — — — — — — — —

I wish to contribute to future SHORTCUTS publications
in the status of a writer-for-hire under the copyright
law and agree to accept a one-time fee of 10¢ a published word. If more than five of my contributions are
published, I will allow my name to be used as a contributor to the work in which they first appear. All
entries that are paid for become the property of Super-
lative House, Inc. I recognize that Bantam Books has no
obligation under this agreement.

_____   _____
        Contributor   Date

    Superlative House, Inc.

By: _____   _____
                                      Date

ABOUT THE EDITORS

TIMOTHY R. AUGELLO is active in art, literature and music. He is an agent for authors and artists and a freelance editorial consultant. He also composes music, designs landscapes and paints. A number of his artworks have been reproduced as greeting cards and posters.

GARY D. YANKER is a practicing attorney and the author of numerous articles and books on how-to, consumer, and self-improvement subjects, including *Improving Yourself*, Dodd, Mead, 1973; *Prop Art*, New York Graphic Society, 1972; *The Angry Buyer's Complaint Directory*, David McKay, 1974. He received a B.A. from Georgetown University, a J.D. from Columbia University School of Law, and an M.B.A. from Columbia University Graduate School of Business Administration. He is a Phi Beta Kappa and a member of the National Business Honor Society (Beta Gamma Sigma). He lectures at Columbia University Graduate School of Business Administration, the New School and New York University Law and Tax Institute. He is an ultramarathoner, who walks, runs and skates distances in excess of 1,000 miles.

THE ONLY INVESTMENT GUIDE
YOU'LL EVER NEED
by Andrew Tobias

No matter how much or how little you have, this bestselling money book is for you. THE ONLY INVESTMENT GUIDE YOU'LL EVER NEED is filled with beneficial tips and angles, such as why you should *not* buy ordinary life insurance, how to save up to 75% in brokerage commissions, how to earn 30% to 40% on everything from mouthwash to tuna fish, and much more. (#14481-2 • $2.75)

184 BUSINESSES ANYONE CAN START
AND MAKE A LOT OF MONEY
by Chase Revel

Chase Revel made his first million by the time he was 21. He has entered into 18 separate ventures and has made a killing at all but one. Now, in this book, he offers 184 easy-to-follow, highly informative business outlines, including possible profits, average investments, special marketing angles and much more—a virtual primer course on becoming a self-made success. Be your own boss! Take control of your life! After reading this book, the only person to blame for a dull, low-paying job is yourself. (A large format book • #01298-3 • $6.95)

We Deliver!

And So Do These Bestsellers.